ON BEING A SHIT

*Unkind Deeds and Cover-Ups
in Everyday Life*

ALSO BY JANE GILGUN

Children's Books

Busjacked!
Emma and her Forever Person
Five Little Cygnets Cross the Bundoran Road
Patrick and the Magic Mountain
The King's Toast
The Little Pig Who Didn't go to Market
The Picking Flower Garden
Turtle Night at Playa Grande
Will the Soccer Star

Books

Child Sexual Abuse: From Harsh Realities to Hope
Children with Serious Conduct Issues
I Want to Show You: Poems
The NEATS: A Child & Family Assessment

Manuals

Lemons or Lemonades? An Anger Workbook for Kids
Leomons or Lemonade? An Anger Workbook for Teens
Readiness to Adopt Children with Special Needs

Jane Gilgun has many articles and assessment tool available on social media websites.

ON BEING A SHIT

*Unkind Deeds and Cover-Ups
in Everyday Life*

Jane F. Gilgun

Createspace
2012

Gilgun, Jane.
On Being a Shit: Unkind Deeds and Cover-ups
in Everyday Life/by Jane Gilgun
revised edition

1. social science 2. self-help 3. humor 4. psychology 5. linguistics
6. research methods. I. Title. 179 pages, including endnotes

ISBN-13: 978-1452873114
ISBN-10: 1452873119

Visit Amazon Kindle, Google Books, iBooks, & other Internet booksellers
to discover other books, articles, and children's stories by Jane Gilgun
that you may enjoy.

ACKNOWLEDGEMENTS

For reading drafts of this book and for their encouragement, I thank Mary Jo Ackerman, Joy Davis, Ray Dull, Ed Foley, Rachelle Goodall, John J. Gilgun, Forrest Pastor, Tina Pommer, Susan Renstrom-Fortney, and Alankaar Sharma. Thanks to John F. Gilgun for honest feedback and to Phyllis Galbraith, Ray Dull, and Sharon Ladin for proofreading. For help with contracts, gratitude to Mary Connelly. To Anita McClellan of McClellan Associates, thanks for her readings of drafts, help with contracts, and ongoing interest.

Special thanks to people I interviewed about family and community violence whose stories helped me to see how common unkind deeds and cover-ups are.

Jane F. Gilgun
Minneapolis, Minnesota, USA
August 30, 2012

Contents

PART TWO

Testing the Theory
on Stories from Everyday Life

PART THREE

Applications of the Theory
to Stories of Coming Clean

On Accountability

PART FOUR

Discussion and Conclusions, or Where Do We Go From Here?

APPENDICES

ONE

Introduction: Sniffing Them Out

When someone dumps on us and then tries to cover-up,
a typical response is "You shit!"

C ara said to her lover Nick when she found out he had been seeing another woman, "What do you want? A harem?" An impish look appeared on Nick's face, and he said, "Two women? That's not much of a harem." Cara laughed, tickled by the charm that endeared Nick to her. With her laugh, Cara's tension lifted, and they talked about other things.

Nick finessed Cara in an elegant, tailor-made way. His involvement with another woman hurt Cara, and he covered up through humor. He had been with Cara long enough to know that a humorous response would distract her and lift her mood. Cara cooperated. She enabled Nick to cover up an unkind deed, in other words, to be a shit.

Katherine Armstrong described as "little bitty pellets" the shotgun blast that Dick Cheney, the vice president of the United States, fired into Harry Whittington while hunting quail on the Armstrong ranch in February 2006. She said that she herself had been shot upon occasion, and Harry was fine, sitting up in his hospital bed, "yakking."

Actually, Harry spent six days in the hospital. A few days after being shot, he had a heart attack when a pellet migrated to his heart.

When Harry left the hospital, he said at a press conference, "My family and I are deeply sorry for all that Vice President Cheney and his family have had to go through this past week. We send our love and respect to them as they deal with situations that are much more serious than what we have had this week.... We hope that he will continue to come to Texas and seek the relaxation that he deserves." With these words, Harry cooperated with the minimization of the vice president's deeds and his own near-death. In doing so, he enabled the vice president to be a shit.

S ophie told her husband Bill, "You're too sensitive" when he gagged at the bits of beef, carrots, and asparagus, along with lumps of toothpaste and bubbles of spit she had left in the bathroom sink after she had brushed her teeth. Sophie's words stung Bill. He instantly felt better when he resolved to leave his own mouth garbage in the sink the next time he brushed his teeth. Too sensitive, my ass. He'll show her.

Sophie not only dismissed Bill's concerns, but she distracted him from her own insensitivity by pointing out something wrong with him. Being called sensitive hit one of Bill's hot buttons. He believed he was too sensitive and was ashamed of that. Rather than let shame eat him up, he vowed to get back at Sophie. When he bought into Sophie's accusation, he enabled her to be shit. By plotting revenge, Bill was on his way to becoming one himself.

Unkind Deeds and Cover-Ups

While differing in their details, these scenarios have much in common. In each of them, someone committed an unkind deed and then tried to cover up through humor, minimization, dismissiveness, and deflection of blame. In the vice president's case, a spokesperson covered up for him. In each instance, recipients bought into the cover-ups. Harry Whittington may have only given the appearance of buy-in, but he spoke the words of someone who enables others to get away with unkind deeds.

On Being a Shit is about such unkind deeds and cover-ups. Instances of being a shit (called BS from here on in) flourish in families, in neighborhoods, at work, and on the highway. The potential for BS exists wherever two or more people congregate. Getting others to believe unkind deeds are their own fault is the crowning achievement of BS.

Unkind deeds and cover-ups extend into politics, business, sports, academic life, and even world affairs. Richard M. Nixon's "I don't recall" cover-up of his knowledge of the Watergate break-in is one of the most famous political cover-ups in the last fifty years. Floyd Landis' alleged doping during the 2006 Tour de France bicycle race and his apparent cover-ups made headlines throughout the world.

The Idea for the Book

For more than twenty-five years, I did research on serious violence, such as rape, child molestation, and murder. In their own words, perpetrators described multiple and ingenious ways they evaded responsibility for their behaviors and, whenever possible, blamed others for their own terrible deeds.

As I became familiar with criminal acts and cover-ups, I began to notice variations of them operating in everyday life among persons who had committed relatively minor unkind deeds and who sought to cover them up through evasion, distortion, and blame.

When I read Harry Frankfurt's best-selling book *On Bullshit*, I found a name for the unkind deeds and cover-ups that I had noticed for so many years. I called these everyday acts *being a shit* and decided to write a book about them. Frankfurt, a philosopher, wrote a philosophical essay. I am a researcher, and the present book is a report on research I conducted.

I chose the impolite *being a shit* over other more respectable terms such as *being insufficiently accountable* and *the evasion of responsibility* because the term *being a shit* fits how we experience unkind deeds and cover-ups in everyday life. When someone dumps on us and then tries to cover it up, a typical response is "You shit!"

I wrote this book to let others know what I have learned from years of research and in so doing to help them avoid being trapped in the maneuvers that are now so familiar to me. With this level of awareness, I freely admit that I have been a recipient of unkind deeds and cover-ups and have expertise in enabling them. I am much better at being a recipient than an enactor, although I have some talent in that regard as well.

I also wrote this book in the hope that those who enact BS will enjoy reading about themselves, until, of course, they get to the parts where they see that I am on to them. Then, I cannot predict what they will do, perhaps ridicule the book so they can carry on. A few may see the light and change their ways.

My fondest hope is that *On Being a Shit* will clue recipients about their parts in the cycle of unkind deeds and cover-ups, and they will opt out of cooperating with the sometimes clever and not-so-clever strategies of cover-up that hook them into believing that false representations are true.

DEVELOPING AND TESTING A THEORY OF BEING A SHIT

In this book, I developed and tested a theory of BS. To do so, I used a method called deductive qualitative analysis. Deductive qualitative analysis (DQA) involves several steps. The first is to write down everything researchers already know about the topic that interests them. The next is to review what others have written about the topic and related issues. Based on what researchers learn from these two steps, they formulate a preliminary theory. Then they test the preliminary theory and change it when there is evidence to do so. The final product is a revised theory that fits the new evidence. Researchers typically do DQA in order to come up with a better, more accurate and trustworthy theory. That was my purpose in developing and testing a theory of BS.

I followed these procedures in the present investigation. I first wrote out my assumptions based upon my own research, my professional experience as a social worker, and observations of everyday life. The results of this effort compose Chapters One and Two. Next, I reviewed scholarly writings on the meanings of the word *shit* and on related topics, such as humbug, bullshit, and lying. I also consulted cognitive neuroscience for insights this discipline might offer. These reviews are in Chapters Three and Four.

I then developed a preliminary theory of BS. This composes Chapter Five. Following that, I tested the theory on a series of cases. The testing is reported in Chapters Six through Nineteen.

In Chapters Twenty through Twenty-Four, I applied the theory to cases where enactors either voluntarily mended their ways or were pressured to do so. Chapter Twenty-Five is a commentary on fake and true accountability. Chapter Twenty-Six shows what not to do when enactors blow back at persons who confront them about their unkind deeds and cover-ups. Chapters Twenty-Seven through Thirty-Two discuss the results of testing the theory.

The results include findings that the preliminary theory did not anticipate, such as the joys of BS and what to call enactors who fail at being shits. These final chapters include a revised and tested theory and a discussion of the implications of the revised theory. Included in the discussion are lessons learned on how to resist the tactics that enactors use to cover up their unkind deeds.

The cases on which I tested the theory are stories about people from many walks of life and who covered up a wide variety of unkind deeds. I chose a diverse sample because I want the theory to be useful in as many different situations as possible. I found that the theory fit most cases well. The theory also helped me to see aspects of BS I might not otherwise have noticed.

This book spoofs social science theory-building. Who ever heard of testing a theory of BS? On the other hand, BS happens so often that it warrants close scientific scrutiny. What's more, this book provides a model of how to do theory testing using qualitative data, something that is of interest to many graduate students and researchers. I hope readers enjoy reading the book as much as I enjoyed writing it and that its contents enlighten them as much as I have been enlightened.

TWO

Shedding Light in Dark Places

*Getting others to believe it is their fault
is the crowning achievement of BS*

N o matter where we go, we run into other people who practice the art and craft of BS. We are awash in execrable behaviors. Everyone contributes to them. They are such a part of everyday life that we fail to notice them and, as a result, take them for granted. Some practitioners have reached that state of perfection where recipients think they are at fault. Getting others to believe it is their fault is the crowning achievement of BS.

BS dates back to antiquity and perhaps to the dawn of human history. The first instance was when a member of a mastodon hunting party threw a lance into the side of another hunter and then scolded the injured man for getting in the way. The injured man immediately saw the distress of the hunter who had caused the injury and said, "My heart goes out to you. You must be distraught that this accident should happen to you. How thoughtless of me to get in the way. I hope you can forgive me."

The spear thrower accepted the apology with grace. The wounded man was filled with gratitude at being forgiven. Since that time, human beings have had an unbroken record of BS.

THREE CATEGORIES OF BS: REACTORS, TRUE BELIEVERS, AND CLEVER FOXES

There are three general categories of BS: Those who react without thinking and are out of touch with the effects of their behaviors on others, those who believe their own concoctions and dismiss the effects of their actions, and those who know exactly what they are doing and enjoy themselves while doing so.

Reactors

Despite humanity's long acquaintance, we know little about BS. Those who react without thinking cannot enlighten because their actions are automatic and happen in the absence of conscious thought. Automatic behaviors may originate in the subconscious, perhaps in as yet unmapped regions of the lower brain, areas referred to as reptilian. Automatic responses by-pass the regions of the brain responsible for reasoning, caring, and and empathy. Often, these responses also by-pass areas of the brain associated with a sense of humor.

Individuals who react without thinking are unable to say why they behave as they do because they have no thoughts to report. When their unkind deeds come to light, their spontaneous responses are blunt, blaming, and loud. They are incapable of insight into their wrongdoings, and they blame others rather than admit they did something wrong. Self-focused and clueless about the effects of their actions on others, they show little caring and empathy for the recipients of their unkind deeds. Finally, they have no sense of humor.

These people are Reactors. Reactors are the least skilled and least reflective of the enactors of BS. Yet, they could be the most common.

True Believers

Those who believe their own concoctions represent the second style of BS. They explain their behaviors at length and think their insights are rare, well-said, and self-evident. Captivated by their own perspectives, they view recipient objections as inappropriate and unjustifiable. When recipients question their unkind deeds, their favored responses are attack and dismissiveness: "You're too sensitive." "Where's your sense of humor?" "I was only kidding." Other typical responses are indignation and even outrage. "How dare you?" "Who do you think you are?" "How can you think such things of me?" They cannot see the points of view of others.

T he thinking parts of their brains are selectively engaged when they are being shits. They tap into reasoning that permits their sometimes elegant explanations, but they avoid digging deeper into themselves to understand their own behaviors and how their behaviors hurt others. In addition, their thought patterns exclude empathy. This makes it hard for them to imagine how others might see things. In short, they have tunnel vision. Thus, they may be confused and even enraged but almost always eloquent when they others challenge them. Their sense of humor is often underdeveloped. As a result, they mistake mockery for wit.

Unlike Reactors who have few or no reasons for why they do what they do, this second type of enactor has explanations that are logical and even elegant to them, but, when viewed with clear eyes, their explanations are partial and distorted. Under these circumstances, they cannot shed light on the true nature of their behaviors and cannot contribute to a theory of BS. Those who operate this way are True Believers.

Clever Foxes

The characteristic behaviors of True Believers are self-deceptive compared to the third type. These are individuals who know exactly what they are doing and enjoy themselves while doing so. Their conscious goal is to deceive others. Not only do they have thought processes that engage the brain's seat of reasoning to a much larger degree than those of True Believers and Reactors, but they also have well-developed capacities for humor, irony, bluffing, bullshit, prevarication, and other higher order talents. Despite these assets, they are deficient in sympathy and compassion.

Some brain circuits are under-developed through lack of use while other circuits are over-developed through frequent use. They have advanced capacities for a special type of empathy in that they have sharp instincts about the vulnerabilities of others, but, instead of sympathizing, they take advantage of these vulnerabilities for their own gain.

These enactors are more complex and some may say more interesting than True Believers and Reactors. This third type is called the Clever Fox

RECIPIENTS AS UNWITTING ENABLERS

On their own, these three types—Reactors, True Believers, and Clever Foxes—cannot accomplish being shits (BS) because attaining that status requires recipients who buy into their cover-ups. Recipients come in more than one variety. Some believe they are responsible for the conduct of others. When enactors blame them, they take the blame. Some others are susceptible to humorous cover-ups, and others fall for cover-ups that play upon their sympathy. Some recipients flounder in confusion when enactors cover up. They are unsure of what is going on and give enactors the benefit of the doubt or think maybe it is them. Others are satisfied with enactors' explanations and are not confused. They think they know what is going on but they do not. Some people have all of these styles of buy-in from time to time, while others have one typical style.

Theories of being a shit (BS) that come from recipients cannot enlighten because enactors have succeeded in hoodwinking them, have led them down the garden path, taken them to the cleaners, duped them, and eaten them for lunch. Any theories recipients construct are based upon the premise that false representations are true.

How Little We Know

The three types of enactors and the many different responses of recipients have only partial views and even these views are distorted. As a result, we know little about BS. We do not know how many different kinds there are, what purposes BS serves, or how BS ties us to and divides us from other people, including people we love and who love us, at least those who love us part time. We have few ideas about how to respond to those who enact unkind deeds and cover-ups.

This present investigation may be the first to develop deeper understandings of being a shit (BS), further testimony to the neglect of this important topic. To develop these deeper understandings, the investigation ranged far and wide as is fitting for such an important and wide-spread issue. The search for understanding followed procedures that have advanced human knowledge in many other realms.

THREE

Scholarly Inquiry
into Origins and Meanings of BS

Shit is one of the most versatile words in the English language

S*hit* as a word has a long and hallowed history in the English language. Many other languages have similar word with the same root, but surprisingly different meanings. Today, its literal meaning is the by-product of digestion and, in technical language, its synonyms are *feces* as a noun and *to defecate* as a verb. These are natural, necessary, and inevitable bodily functions.

The word comes from the Latin verb *scire*, to know, or "to separate one thing from another." This is its root meaning, as in *discern*, which means to separate something out from a larger picture, such as focusing on Mona Lisa's smile rather than her entire face. Other contemporary English words related to the root word include *schism, scissors, science, omniscient, schizophrenic, rescind, scatological*, and *shed*.

Related words appear in many other ancient languages, such as Old English *scinu*, shin, shinbone, meaning "piece cut off," in Middle Dutch and Middle Low German as *schive*, a slice, and Greek *skhizein*, to split.

As meaning *feces* and *to defecate*, similar words appear in Old Norse as the word *skīta*, as *scitte* in Old English, *schitte* in Middle English, *skit* in Proto-Germanic, and *skheid* in Proto-European, a language that is the root of several contemporary Germanic languages, such as Swedish, Dutch, and German. In Ireland, *shit* may sometimes be pronounced as *skit*, retaining the older pronunciations of its root word.

The Versatility of the Word

Shit is among the most versatile words in the English language and is used as a noun, adjective, verb, adverb, and exclamation to express affection, anger, joy, pride, shame, empathy, and many other emotional states. Its meanings depend on the contexts in which it is used.

Here are some examples. Jay and Sylvia were parked in Lover's Lane deep in the Ozarks of southern Missouri. Jay said, "I love you, girl." Sylvia replied, "Oh, shit" (joy, affection, adoration, exclamation). She pronounced it "she-it."

As an exclamation, the word has additional meanings, as, for example, when Mary said to Jane, "I got a D on the chemistry exam." Jane said, "Oh, shit, Mary. I'm sorry" (sympathy). Other meanings as exclamations are common. Cathy banged her head on the sink as she started to stand after scrubbing the bathroom floor. She said, "Shit!" (exasperation, pain). Bjorn left the bathroom with toilet paper stuck to his foot. His older brother Pete laughed at him. Bjorn said, "Oh, shit" (embarrassment).

A Noun with Many Meanings

Shit as a noun has many meanings. Alex said to Marty, "You don't know jack shit about that" (insult). Rose bragged to Annie, her next door neighbor, about her four year-old son Johnny, "He's a cute little shit, don't you think?" (pride, endearment). Tina said to Seamus about a neighbor who brought in heavy equipment to dig a well at 5:30 am on a Sunday morning, "He's such a shit" (contempt).

The word can also refer to activities as when Mabel said to Charlie when she found out he was running around with other women: "Don't you pull that shit on me. I know what you're up to" (bad behavior). It can also refer to objects and things, as when Teenie the buyer asked Smoky the dope dealer, "Got any good shit today?" (something good) and the following week said, "What kind of shit did you sell me last week? I passed out after my first toke" (something bad).

Shit can have a broader meaning, such as when it refers to an entire life. Rocky, who felt down and out, said, "I've got to get my shit together" (everything in my life).

Sometimes the word is part of a compound noun. Grandma Bridget said to her son Brian about finding money missing from her purse after her adult grandson Robert visited her in the nursing home: "He's such a shitass." *Shitass* is a variation of the more common term *shithead.* When Kylie and James heard what Grandma had said, they laughed. They could not imagine that their sweet great grandmother would use that word.

As Modifier

As a modifier, *shit* has limitless possibilities. Paul told his buddies about seeing a panda on the ninth hole when golfing in China: "I was scared shitless" (fear). Teacher Fran read Alfie's essay and said to herself, "That's a pretty shitty effort" (bad job). Jim to Jack, "How'd it go?" "Pretty shitty," Jack answered (didn't go well).

Meanings in Other Countries

Other English-speaking countries uses the word in many different ways. In Irish, Scottish, and British English, *shit* may be spelled *shite* and pronounced to rhyme with *white. Shite* refers to any object, entity, or thing that is crap, schlock, or pap, quite similar to some of the meanings of American English *shit.*

Pádraig Clancy, an Irish football player, used the word to express his exasperation with criticism sports writers had given him for bragging about how brilliantly he would play in an upcoming game. Pádraig said, "I wouldn't have any time for that shite, to plaster me on the back of a paper two days before the match." Pádraig's team lost.

The word had a starring role at a meeting of the world's leading economic powers at the Group of 8 Summit held in St.

Petersburg, Russia, in July 2006. At the closing luncheon, not knowing that a microphone was still on, George W. Bush, president of the United States, said with his mouth full, "What they [unclear who 'they' refers to] need to do is get Syria to get Hezbollah to stop doing this shit, and it's over." He was talking to Tony Blair, prime minister of the United Kingdom.

A few days later, a cartoon in the newspaper *Newsday* showed the prime minister correcting the president in his pronunciation of the word *shit*: "Actually, George, it's pronounced *'shite.'*"

SOCIAL CONVENTIONS

Despite the incredible number of ways that speakers of English use the term *shit,* few scholars have studied what it means to be a shit. Its status as a vulgarism may account for this neglect. Dictionaries, when they have an entry at all, almost universally note that the word is slang, part of the vernacular, vulgar, not used in polite company and formal speech.

Even when the word itself is the subject of a news story, newspapers are inconsistent in their use of the term. The *New York Times*, in a front page article on George W. Bush's use of *shit*, did not print the term itself but called it a "vulgarity," "undiplomatic prose," and "locker-room banter." A few days later, in Thomas Friedman's column, the *Times* printed the word in its entirety. Many other newspapers, both in the U.S. and internationally used the word with no apologies, as did countless bloggers.

The print media were ingenious in their avoidance of the word in reviews of Harry Frankfurt's book, *On Bullshit*. A southern newspaper reported the title as "On Bull--." A west coast newspaper evaded the word in several ways, including "the yuk-promising title On [Word-We-Can't-Print-in-Family-Newspaper]," the "word in question" as "the equivalent of 'bull hockey,'" and "B.S." An eastern paper described the term "an unprintable ubiquity" and referred to the book as "On Bull----"

as it did more than a year later when it published a review of the sequel to *On Bullshit*, called *On Truth*.

In summary, social conventions are powerful enough to wipe *shit* from the pages of some newspapers, but these conventions are not respected world-wide. The status of *shit* as slang and a vulgarity may account for its absence from philosophical and other scholarly discussions. Books like Frankfurt's and the present investigation spoof these conventions.

Restoring the Word to Respectability

Shit was not always a vulgarism. The word became unmentionable in the nineteenth century, a time when embarrassment about natural body functions was a mark of refinement within some social classes. Many of the terms used for these functions became offensive. At that time, the word *leg* was an unmentionable. The proper term for *leg of a table* was *limb of a table*.

My investigation into what it means to be a shit might restore the word to respectability. This would have the benefit of freeing up the use of a term that fits many aspects of family, community, and political life. Recipients cannot bring their experiences of unkind deeds and cover-ups into wide-spread public discussion because they cannot use the language that springs spontaneously to mind. The word's status as rude and impolite deprives recipients of their natural language. When individuals cannot use words that fit their experiences, they are forced to be silent. As a result, enactors of unkind deeds and cover-ups are free to carry on.

The Search for a More Suitable Word

Since the term *shit* may offend some readers, I searched for a more suitable word, but in vain. I considered the word *weasel*. *Weasel* connotes a sneaky, underhanded way of wiggling out of taking responsibility for unkind deeds and thus evading accountability. As I tried the word out, I saw that being a weasel refers to a narrow range of behaviors and could be part of the broader category of BS.

Schmuck

Next I examined *schmuck,* which means being a jerk, or a stupid, foolish, and often obnoxious person. Its synonym is *putz,* as in "He (or she) is a true schmuck, a putz." These words are associated with the male gender, but in some situations they fit the behaviors of women. I found the meanings of these terms too limited for the present investigation and realized that being a schmuck or putz, like the term *weasel,* could be a subcategory of BS. Both *schmuck* and *putz* are derived from High German and are part of Yiddish slang whose root meaning refers to a lower body part, namely, the penis, as does the next term I considered.

Prick

Prick had some promise. *Prick* means to puncture, or to stick a sharp point into something, such as the prick of a needle. The root word is the Old English *prica,* which means a puncture, possibly related to a West Germanic word *prikk-.* The word has many meanings including those associated with emotions, such as to goad, as in "My conscience pricked me into action" and with other mildly painful emotions denoting a stinging sensation, as in the *"prick of regret."*

Prick is both a nautical term as "pricking a course on a chart" and a term used in horticulture as a synonym for "setting out," as in "pricking out seedlings before they are transplanted into a permanent place." "To prick up the ears" refers to paying attention to something, an action common to dogs, horses, and other mammals that have ears they can move. In many contexts, then, *prick* has no whiff of vulgarity.

In the past, the word *prick* described the gallop of horses, such as "The horse pricked across the desert." In seventeenth and eighteenth century English, *prick* meant a pimple, which may account for its status as a term of endearment, as in "He's a cute little prick," similar to "She's a cute little shit." *Prick* at one time was associated with professionals who prick others, as in *pricksmith*, which, during the Second World War, meant an Army medical office, especially those assigned to dealing with venereal diseases. A "prick-parade" stood for the inspections that these medical officers conducted.

Prick's Meanings Today

Today, the term refers to both *penis* and an *obnoxious person.* Another sense of the word refers to persons who lie to themselves and others in a misguided attempt to salvage their pride. Such was the situation in the 1999 film Notting Hill where William Thacker, played by Hugh Grant, longed for the love of Anna Scott, played by Julia Roberts. When Anna finally declared her love for him, William turned her away. He preferred false pride to immediate acceptance of her love. When he realized what he had done, he called himself a prick.

The word *prick* as standing for penis appears to have been part of standard English until the eighteenth century when it became a vulgarism. The word *prick-teaser*, whose meaning is self-evident to most people, is unlikely ever to have been part of standard English.

The meaning of *prick*, then, is versatile, but not to the same degree as the word *shit.* Despite its versatility, *shit* is a more fitting term for the present purposes, primarily because that word fits so well the experience of being a recipient of unkind deeds and cover-ups. Not only do many people use that word in spontaneous responses to being dumped on, but those who enact being shits are successful because their actions lead recipients to feel as if they are shit. In fact, a way to detect shit is to notice when you feel like shit. Chances are someone has just dumped on you.

Both *prick* and *shit* are associated with the male gender, and only males have the body part associated with *prick.* Both genders, however, have capacities to engage in behaviors to which *shit* refers, another advantage of sticking with the word.

THE UNSUITABILITY OF ABSTRACT TERMS

Besides these everyday terms, I considered others that are more abstract, such as *accountability* and *taking responsibility*. These terms have similar meanings. Both mean capacities to explain one's actions in a truthful way and to take responsibility for the consequences of one's actions. True accountability and taking of responsibility mean that individuals recognize that they are free agents capable of choice. Furthermore, accountable persons accept the consequences of their own actions, do not blame others, otherwise try to excuse themselves, or cover up their behaviors.

These terms are sterile in contrast to the earthy meanings and guttural sound of the word *shit,* and they do not have the impact that fits the experience of being a recipient of unkind deeds and cover-ups. For recipients, unkind deeds and cover-ups are not abstractions, but are visceral, experienced in the body. They cause aches in the gut and heart, a dizziness of the spirit where the actions of others lead one to believe that one has done something wrong, but is at a loss as to what that might be.

Being a recipient of unkind deeds and cover-ups leads many to be struck dumb because of being caught between what one expects from another and what the other delivers. The more abstract terms do not fit the experience of what it means to be a recipient of shit.

The terms *lack of responsibility* or *insufficient accountability* are much discussed in scholarly journals and books related to criminology where researchers apply them to the crimes and misdemeanors that led to arrests, trials, and upon conviction, probation, jail, or prison time, not to mention social stigma and shame. Pleading guilty to criminal acts may result in lighter sentences, which indicates the value the criminal justice system puts on accountability. Refusals to be accountable for criminal behaviors are forms of unkind deeds and cover-ups that are against the law.

CONCLUSIONS: BS
APPEARS IN MANY DIFFERENT FORMS

In summary, my review of relevant scholarship did not identify a term that conveys unkind deeds and cover-ups in everyday life with the simplicity and directness that I seek. So, I am content with the simple, homey, and perhaps vulgar *shit*.

The present inquiry into the history and meanings of the term can be summarized in a few sentences. The word has multiple meanings. Variations appear in many ancient and modern languages. There appears to be no other term that conveys so plainly what it means to enact and cover up unkind deeds.

BS as Complicated

When I began this inquiry, I had hoped that being a shit would be easy to spot. Related scholarship has shown that this may not be so. There simply are too many ways that the word is used.

I am beginning to suspect that being a shit is ever-changing, like the Greek god of the sea Proteus who knew the truth about everything but resisted telling what he knew by changing shape, as from snake, to seal, to fish, to bird, etc. Only when absolutely forced did he say what he knew to be the truth.

Realizing that shit may be a word whose meanings change suggested that it may be impossible to pin down the nature of BS. When we think we have it, it changes shape. On the other hand, a simple and clear theory could cut through surface differences and pull out the core of what it means to be a shit.

Summary

Human beings have succeeded at being shits since the dawn of human history. Those who enact being shits come in three varieties: reactive, self-focused, or clever—in other words, Reactors, True Believers, or Clever Foxes. Recipients believe that those who enact unkind deeds and cover-ups act in good faith, when in actuality enactors do all they can to evade responsibility, including blaming others, even people they love.

Recipients may be hoodwinked and believe they are responsible for the unkind deeds and cover-ups that others enact, or they have feel as if done something wrong. They ask, "Is it me?" When recipients figure out what enactors have done, they may exclaim privately, "What a shit!" or "You shit!" But they cannot use such language in a public way and participate in a public discussion because their natural language has an aura of vulgarity, unmentionability, and rudeness. Robbed of their natural language, recipients may be silenced. When recipients are silenced, enactors can carry on. Such a state of affairs shows the urgency of developing and testing a theory of BS.

FOUR

Humbug, Bullshit, Lying, and Truthiness: Conditions Related to BS

BS differs from related conditions

T he next step in theory development is to become familiar with research and theory on related topics. This often results in discovering new dimensions of the area of interest as well as learning what something is not. These procedures are similar to prospecting for gold, seeking to separate the real thing from the sand, pebbles, and pyrite, in the hopes that eventually, the qualities of BS will shine forth.

Other scholars have done research on topics similar to BS, but not on BS itself. These topics include humbug, bullshit, lying, and truthiness. In addition, cognitive neuroscience may contribute important ideas to a theory of BS.

HUMBUG

Humbug is a deliberate form of deception that is a self-important use of someone else's words, thoughts, feelings, or actions. Humbug "falls short of lying," according to philosophy professor Harry Frankfurt, author of *On Bullshit*, a text mentioned earlier. Its intent is not to deceive but to produce in others a favorable impression of oneself.

Humbug conjures up images of pompous men who speak endlessly on an open-air dais on the patriotic theme of the day. Uttering humbug is a kind of game that most everyone understands, although recipients may be bored into stupefaction, not because of the subject matter but because of the self-puffery of its delivery.

BULLSHIT

Some of the characteristics of bullshit are similar to those of humbug. Like humbug, bullshit is not lying. It can have humorous effects and involve misrepresentations intended to create a certain image of the bullshitter. As a result, bullshit is unconnected to literal truth and remains, in Frankfurt's words, indifferent "to how things really are." One who bullshits is "trying to get away with something," wrote Frankfurt, possibly to have fun with others. In contrast, those who speak humbug want to puff themselves up by association with noble causes.

From my point of view, persons who engage in bullshit do not expect to be held to their ideas and opinions because of an implicit understanding that bullshitters are uncommitted to the truth. Those who speak humbug, on the other hand, strive to have others take them seriously. By definition, they do not succeed.

LYING

Lies, like humbug and bullshit, are misrepresentation, but lies differ from bullshit and humbug because individuals who lie know what the truth is and want to conceal it. Like humbug and bullshit, lies are a means of creating and managing impressions. They are attempts to imitate the truth, with the key word being *imitate* since individuals who lie want only to give the appearance of truth.

Lies of Commission and Omission

Paul Ekman, known for his research on lying and the detection of deception, identified two types of lies. The first is the concealment of information and the second is the falsification of information. In concealment, individuals withhold the truth and know they are doing so. One of his examples was Hitler's withholding of information from Neville Chamberlain, prime minister of the United Kingdom, in September 1938 about his intention to invade Czechoslovakia.

Hitler gave his word that he would not attack Czechoslovakia if that country met his demands. Chamberlain believed Hitler and advised the Czechs to work something out with Hitler. This bought Hitler time to get his army ready. Hitler subsequently attacked Czechoslovakia, whose leaders had also taken Hitler for his word. After the invasion, Chamberlain said he had thought Hitler to be a man of his word. The falsification of information involves "barefaced lies" where individuals make up something that is untrue. Falsification usually arises from a motivation to conceal something.

Intermediate between concealment and falsification is the memory failure strategy. In 1973, White House chief of staff Alexander Haig advised President Richard M. Nixon to evade questions about Nixon's knowledge of the Watergate break-in by saying he could not recall. The three strategies of concealment, falsification, and memory failure are, of course, forms of lying. Some commentators call falsifications lies of commission and concealments lies of omission.

Little Lies and Big Lies

Most lies do not inflict harm, and these are called little lies, fibs, or white lies. Their purposes range from self-centered, such as to protect the self from disapproval, to altruistic, as in protecting others from information that might upset them. An example of the latter is a person who tells a parent how adorable a toddler is when in fact the child is demanding and rude.

In contrast to little lies, big lies are attempts to deceive about matters that would aggrieve, hurt, or anger the persons who are recipients. Dating someone else's boyfriend, stealing from your grandmother, and teens having a party when parents are away are examples. In politics, invading another country or presidential dirty tricks are additional examples.

Research on Little and Big Lies

Researchers Bella DePaulo and Deborah Kashy asked almost one hundred and fifty people to keep a diary for one week in which they recorded the lies they told. The researchers defined lies as "any time you intentionally try to mislead someone," where "both the intent to deceive and the actual deception must occur" either through words or actions.

By week's end, the participants reported that they had lied a fifth to a third of the time in their conversations with others. They were more likely to tell little lies to strangers and acquaintances and more serious lies to persons with whom they felt close.

DePaulo and Kashy found that when participants started to tell little lies to persons with whom they were intimate, this often signaled a decrease in intimacy. The researchers also found that persons who lied felt more distress before and after lying to casual friends than to persons who were intimates.

Both big and little lies result in discomfort that DePaulo called a "smudge," which is a kind of "smarmy feeling" once individuals have lied. This discomfort could be a sign of a guilty conscience and might prick some who have lied to come clean.

Responses of Recipients to Lies

In research on lying that asked participants to report the most serious lie they had ever told and the most serious lie anyone had ever told them, DePaulo and colleagues found that when the truth emerged, those who were recipients of lies responded with anger and sadness that included crying, depression, and expressions of hurt feelings. Recipients rarely had loving and forgiving reactions, except when the lies were meant to protect them. Even then recipients typically were hurt and angry, as when loved ones withheld news of the true nature of a parent's illness.

Unmasked liars were more likely to express guilt (apologize, act guilty, ask for forgiveness) than any other reaction, such as "relief (felt relief, wanted to tell)" and "sadness (cried, acted hurt and depressed)," and "happiness (joked, acted happy)." The consequences of lies include loss of trust and intimacy and even the end of relationships.

Successful Lying Requires Skill

Ekman believes that effective lying requires sophisticated cognitive, emotional, and behavioral skills and is composed of three parts: 1) capacities to think strategically, plan ahead, and anticipate consequences, 2) empathic skills that facilitate knowing what others want and need, similar to the advanced skills of some psychotherapists, and 3) capacities for emotion regulation to the point where those who lie mask their emotions and as a result fool others as to what they are actually feeling.

Skilled liars, then, are accomplished human beings, and lying well is dependent upon gifts that not all human beings possess. To be able to think strategically is a sign of well-developed executive functions that involve capacities for planning, organization, self-control, anticipation of consequences, and problem-solving.

The empathic skills of accomplished therapists require years of preparation and practice and a high degree of development in several areas of the human brain, some of which neuroscientists have not yet identified and mapped. At the minimum, the brain regions involved include the neocortex, the amygdala which is one site of emotion, the hippocampus which involves memory functions, and the cingulate gyrus which is associated with knowledge of one's own inner states and the inner states of others. The cingulate gyrus is considered the seat of caring that adults have for children and adults have for each other. It is known for its sensitivity to cues that others want cuddling, nuzzling, and grooming.

The regulation of emotions is a life-long task. Parents and other caring persons teach infants and young children how to manage their emotions so that as time goes by maturing individuals can take on that job themselves. Some human beings are more adept than others in managing their emotions, but most people have trouble when stressed and could react automatically with strong emotions, mixed-up thinking, and agitated behaviors. In other words stress is a risk for dysregulation.

To lie well is to be cool, to think clearly, to have empathic skills to spot the vulnerabilities of others, and to regulate emotions, behaviors, and thoughts in such ways that facial expressions and other non-verbal behaviors do not give away what is really going on.

Recipients as Dupes

When people get away with lies, they have successfully hoodwinked their recipients. Ekman believes that some recipients, whom he calls *dupes*, may be genuinely fooled, and others collude for a long list of reasons. Chief among these reasons are naiveté, desire to avoid conflict, and refusal to believe that others would lie, a state of being called *denial*. In denial, deep down, recipients suspect the truth but in their conscious minds they accommodate to what they want to believe.

For example, Alicia, a wife and mother, made a huge amount of money as a part-time prostitute. Her husband Tom did not know about her occupation and did not question how she got the money. The couple owned a spacious home in an affluent suburb. Both were prominent in local civic affairs, Tom on the park board and Alicia on the city council. When Alicia left the house in the evening, she would say she had a meeting, which she did, but sometimes she met with paying customers. The couple's obvious prosperity was a source of pride for Tom who was widely admired for providing so well for his family. Tom may have wondered how Alicia came up with so much cash, but he did not ask. He may have thought she gambled secretly and won frequently.

Besides showing the benefits that come from going along with lies, this example also shows lies of omission, where Alicia held back information that would contribute to a true and accurate account. She also prevaricated. Prevarications are statements with more than one meaning, one of which is literally true, such as Alicia's statement about going to meetings.

Few People Can Detect Deceit

Few people, even those who are trained as therapists or police investigators, can detect deceit. To use Ekman's term, few people are skilled "lie catchers." Lovers, family members, and close friends are particularly susceptible to believing lies. Liars get away with lying to people who love them because love is based on trust. They expect people they love to tell the truth. Expectations can blind recipients to deceptions.

THE AUTOMATIC ACTIVATION OF SCHEMAS

Cognitive neuroscience provides additional ideas about how easy it can be to fool others. Simply by using particular words, tone of voice, or body language, enactors can evoke automatic responses in recipients in the form of images, thoughts, and feelings. For example, the word *wuss* can conjure up images of a weak, passive person, while *Rambo* brings up images of a muscled hero.

These responses are signs of the activation of schemas, which are mental maps or inner representations of self, others, and how the world works. Schemas are stored in the brain. When activated, they travel along circuits that connect different parts of the brain to each other. As human beings acquire experience, we store uncountable amounts of information in our brains. Over time, words that we used to have to look up in dictionaries now become part of our personal dictionaries that we can recall instantly.

The same is true for speech and actions. For example, the first time children drink out of a cup unassisted, they may have to work and think hard to get the job done. After a while, they perform these actions with ease, without having to think through every step. Learning a new language is another example. At first, the learner's speech is slow and labored, but with long-term experience in hearing and speaking the language, learners become proficient and speak with ease and even dream in this new language. They have developed schemas that activate themselves automatically. They now can do this formerly difficult task without conscious effort. With practice and innate ability, human beings can become proficient at any number of tasks that may have been challenging at the outset.

Schemas and Hot Buttons

We have multitudes of schemas stored in our brains. Each helps us perform the many tasks that we do throughout the day. The situation at hand evokes certain schemas and not others. It is as if human beings are like the keys and buttons of a pipe organ. When a particular key or button is pushed, images, thoughts, and feelings start playing in our minds. The sight of food to hungry people sets off schemas that differ from schemas that activate themselves when the same people are doing housework.

Some of these buttons have little emotional charge and are neutral. For example, in the morning, the sight of a toothbrush and toothpaste evokes schemas that lead to teeth brushing. Some of the buttons evoke warm feelings and happy memories, such as the schemas that activate themselves when a loved one smiles. These buttons are sweet spots. Tom may experience an inner glow when friends and neighbors compliment him on his lovely home. Some buttons set off cold schemas, that is, thoughts, emotions, and memories linked to persons and events that individuals want to avoid but that have no emotional charge.

Some buttons have strong emotional charges and are hot. They set off a torrent of painful emotions and memories. When Cara learned that Nick had been seeing someone else, this hit a hot button. Being called "too sensitive" hit one of Bill's. If Tom had ever learned the truth about Alicia's part-time occupation, we can assume that so many hot buttons would go off that he would be at risk for a stroke. Hot buttons set off emotional, cognitive, and physiological dysregulation.

THROWING LIE-CATCHERS OFF THE SCENT

Ekman briefly addressed excuses liars make when they suspect that they are about to be caught. They may attempt to throw lie catchers off the scent by faking self-righteousness, indignation, and hurt. Another favored tactic is to act as if they are unaware that lie catchers are suspicious so as to "gain time to cover their tracks, prepare an escape, etc."

Like other researchers on lying, Ekman found that persons under suspicion of lying may be uneasy. Some show "detection apprehension" and "deception guilt." He also identified "duping delight," an emotional charge that comes from putting something over on someone else. How liars experience lying may depend upon what is at stake and who is lying to whom. The same enactors could feel afraid of being caught, smarmy, guilty, or delighted depending on the circumstances.

TRUTHINESS

According to the American Dialect Society, truthiness is "the quality of stating concepts or facts one wishes to be true, rather than concepts or facts known to be true." As the Society's 2005 word of the year, truthiness was popularized by Stephen Colbert, the political satirist, on his television show The Colbert Report.

Colbert was concerned that in American politics, there was widespread disregard for facts. He noted that individuals are entitled to their opinions, but they are not entitled to their own facts. Yet, he said, that is exactly what has been happening. Facts no longer matter, but perceptions do.

He used President George W. Bush as a case in point. He said that people love the president because he is certain of the choices he makes, even when he does not have the facts to back up his choices. He wondered what the American people think is more important—what they want to be true or what is true.

Colbert thought he had invented the term, but it had appeared in dictionaries long before he used it. What Colbert did was create new meanings. The meanings in dictionaries are variations of the word *truth*, which is far from what Colbert meant.

Truthiness and Spin

Spin is putting one's own interpretations on events. Katherine Armstrong did some spinning when she said that the pellets Vice President Cheney sprayed into Harry Whittington were "little bitty." Those who spin typically give the appearance of calm sincerity and certainty that individuals who do not agree are nitwits—or unpatriotic. Like truthiness, spin long enough and the spin becomes perception that many people mistake for truth.

The difference between spin and truthiness is that with spin the facts are not contested, and the interpretations are. In contrast, those who speak truthiness overlook facts. In some cases, speakers of truthiness may be the only ones with knowledge of the facts, and they choose to conceal them while pretending to tell the whole truth.

Surprisingly, neither Colbert, the American Dialect Society, nor other commentators saw a connection between truthiness and cover-up. Experienced enactors of cover-up have used truthiness routinely, even when they did not have a name for it. How simple it is for individuals to cover up unkind deeds through giving their versions of events, versions free of facts. Truthiness is similar to prevarication, which are statements that have more than one meaning. Typically, the literal meaning of a prevarication is true. Like truthiness, prevarication has a passing acquaintance with actual events but those who prevaricate know what is true, and they know they are being deceptive when their statements have more than one meaning. In their guile, prevaricators are Clever Foxes. In most cases, speakers of truthiness are, too.

SUMMARY AND DISCUSSION

Research on humbug, bullshit, lying, and truthiness fleshes out what I have learned from research, professional practice, and everyday observations. Frankfurt's work showed that BS is not the same as humbug or bullshit because unkind deeds hurt others, and humbug and bullshit do not.

Ekman's research on lying showed how difficult it is to detect deceit. He noted that professional lie catchers need special training to be effective. The delight that some liars take in duping others may also be a by-product of unkind deeds and cover-ups. The notions of "smudge" and "smarmy" feelings after lying that DePaulo and colleagues identified and Ekman's idea of detection apprehension are likely to earn their way into a theory of BS.

I was surprised to learn that many people whose lies are found out confess and promise repentance. My research and experience suggest that this is rare, but I may have based my assumptions on a sample weighted with people who are strongly motivated to cover up, such as people who are physically and sexually assaultive whom I interviewed for my research on violence. What's more, I have never thought of accomplished liars as skilled human beings despite my notion of Clever Fox. Ekman has spent years studying deception. He knows how sophisticated lying can be.

Research on lying provides two ideas about recipients that could be useful. One is the idea that trust predisposes people to believe cover-ups. The other is that sometimes recipients want to believe the cover-ups because not believing them has too high a price.

Brain research provides additional insights. Success at BS appears to depend up the activation of recipients' hot buttons. If, for example, recipients have hot buttons that trigger over-responsibility for the behaviors of others, it is easy to get them to take responsibility for someone else's unkind deeds. Because they are so good at spotting hot buttons, Clever Foxes may have particularly well-wired brains. Even True Believers, when they can put forth elegant and elaborate explanations for their behaviors, deserve recognition for how well their brains work, although in a distorted kind of way. Overall, this review of related conditions has led to the identification of potentially important ideas for a theory of BS.

FIVE

A Preliminary Theory

*BS is impossible
without the consent of recipients*

I have now completed the work required for the development of a preliminary theory. I have written down my ideas based on my own research, professional experience, and observations of everyday life. I have researched the many meanings of the word *shit*. I have consulted research and theory on related topics. Using these sources, I constructed the following theory.

BS is composed of four parts:

1. an unkind deed
2. a desire to avoid responsibility for the unkind deed
3. a cover-up, and
4. recipient buy-in.

UNKIND DEEDS

The first part, unkind deeds, are everyday acts that hurt someone else. Everyone hurts other people, but what tips hurtful behaviors toward being those of a shit is the refusal to be accountable for unkind deeds.

DESIRE TO GET THE SELF OFF THE HOOK

Refusal of responsibility, or the desire to get the self off the hook, is the second and necessary condition for BS. Desire to get the self off the hook involves actions intended to direct attention away from the self and to anywhere else as long as the person avoids being viewed as being at fault.

Impression Management

One motivation to get the self off the hook is impression management, meaning that enactors want to maintain the appearance of virtue even as they engage in wrongdoings that profit them in some way. Related to impression management is the desire to save face, where unkind deeds put enactors at risk for public shame. Both involve a whitewash of the wrongs that enactors committed.

An example of whitewash is the cover-up that the director of an international bank engineered. He had violated the rules of ethics by giving a job to his live-in companion. As a result, he was at high risk for public disgrace. His board of directors could offer him the face-saving act of resigning instead of being fired. If the director were a Clever Fox, he would refuse to resign until the board agreed to make a public statement that "mistakes were made all around" and to list the fired director's accomplishments during the time he held the job. The reasons for his ouster would not be mentioned. The directors would collude in the cover-up, perhaps as an expedient way to get rid of him

K eeping one's gains is another motivation for cover-up. The gains can be enormous, such as access to wealth, social standing, and personal gratification. Enactors do not want to lose what their unkind deeds have won them.

As a result, desire to avoid consequences keeps fuels the maintenance of unkind deeds and cover-ups. Consequences can take many forms including rejection by family and friends, loss of social standing, public scorn, and financial hardship. By not admitting unkind deeds, enactors apparently believe they can minimize or escape consequences.

Ironically, not being accountable can contribute to the very consequences enactors want to avoid. A sincere and well-timed apology after committing unkind deeds can build relationships and even make them stronger. A refusal to take responsibility can create barriers between people.

Cover-ups come in many varieties, but the motivations behind such behaviors are similar, namely, to keep the gains made through unkind deeds, desires for impression management, for saving face, for getting the self off the hook, and for the evasions of consequences. Floyd Landis is an example of someone who lost a great deal when his cover-ups failed. Floyd won the 2006 Tour de France, but was charged with doping, fired from his team, and stripped of his title when tests showed that he had used illegal drugs. He was banned from bike racing for two years, his reputation ruined.

COVER-UP

The third component of BS is the cover-up. Cover-ups are lies that involve withholding of pertinent facts, making up falsehoods, prevarications, and truthiness. The seriousness of cover-ups ranges from minor to those that are illegal and even lethal. Cover-ups come in two general types: soft and harsh.

Soft Cover-Ups

In soft cover-ups, recipients may not know they have been had. Not only that, but they may end up feeling sorry for enactors. Machiavelli in *The Prince,* a Renaissance guidebook for politicians that is much read today, recommended "soft" cover-ups in the form of duplicity, such as shedding a few tears or putting on other virtuous facades after committing harmful acts that gain and maintain political power and control. Machiavelli stated that deceitful individuals will find a large supply of people to deceive because people are simple of thought and caught up in their own immediate needs.

In both politics and personal affairs, enactors use soft cover-ups. Dick Cheney's soft cover-ups of his shooting of Harry Whittington show how recipients can have more empathy for enactors' trials than their own. Nick's use of humor when Cara asked him about his affair is another soft cover-up that worked. "Two women? That's not much of a harem." In so few words, Nick also minimized his wrongdoing and diffused a hot situation.

George W. Bush used body language and a laugh to cover up his broadcasting the word *shit* during lunch at a meeting of the world's leaders. When his aide showed him the transcripts, he rolled his eyes and laughed, which diffused the situation. Whether this really happened is known only to a few, but it is the story that White House spokespeople put out to the news media who blasted it around the world. Such a story could be truthiness at work.

Harsh Cover-Ups

These soft maneuvers stand in contrast to more harsh measures, such as shaming, blaming and name-calling. Calling Bill too sensitive was a harsh cover-up because Sophie knew that Bill was ashamed of his emotional tenderness. Saying "You asked for it" and "What do you expect?" are other forms of harsh cover-ups when recipients object to enactors' unkind deeds.

Cover-ups and Moral Imagination

Many cover-ups, especially those of the Clever Fox variety, require the empathy of a trained therapist, the talents Ekman attributed to skilled liars, as discussed earlier. The meaning of the term *empathy* goes beyond capacities for identifying the vulnerabilities of others and includes sympathizing and even a desire to comfort.

True empathy requires a moral imagination, according to Alexander McCall Smith, a professor of medical law at the University of Edinburgh, Scotland. He stated that "Morality depends upon an understanding of the feelings of others." To those without moral imagination, Smith wrote, "The pain, the suffering, the unhappiness of others would not seem real, because it would not be perceived."

Thus, Sophie has a special kind of empathy for Bill's sensitivity, but instead of treading lightly, she attacked him where she knew he was vulnerable. Harsh cover-ups result from a lack of moral imagination.

Collateral Damage

Cover-ups, especially those of the harsh type, are harmful to others, but the harm may be an unintended consequence of single-minded determination to attain goals. If they perceive harm at all, enactors may dismiss it as collateral damage. A cover-up that results in collateral damage is the theme of Match Point, a 2005 movie that Woody Allen wrote and directed. The main character, Chris, committed two terrible deeds. He murdered his pregnant mistress and the mistress's neighbor. His mistress had threatened to disclose her relationship with Chris to his wife, who also was pregnant, and to his in-laws.

The family Chris had married into was wealthy and had a high social standing. They thought well of Chris and gave him a job in their company, where he received promotions and a huge salary for his excellent work. Until his marriage, Chris had been a tennis instructor who could barely pay his rent. Chris had a lot to lose if his mistress got in touch with family members.

In his plan to cover up the murder of his mistress, Chris showed the ingenuity and forethought of a Clever Fox. He would burglarize the flat of his mistress's neighbor who was an older woman he had met previously and take jewelry and other small items as evidence of a burglary. The murder of the mistress would take place in the hallway, to give the impression that the mistress had interrupted the burglary and was murdered as a result.

Unfortunately for the neighbor, she arrived back at her flat while Chris was still there. Chris murdered her because she knew who he was. When his mistress arrived home from work, he murdered her in the hallway as he had planned.

Allen used the term *collateral damage* when he had the older woman appear to Chris in a hallucinatory episode to ask him why he had murdered her. Chris showed momentary remorse through his facial expressions and then responded, "You were collateral damage."

The police suspected Chris of both murders but ultimately decided he was not guilty. Chris therefore evaded accountability before the law and also maintained the impression in his family that he was a talented and worthy husband, prospective father, and son in-law. His cover-ups, both pre-planned and spontaneous, worked.

Also, Chris was lucky. The neighbor's ring that he stole to feign a burglary and then threw away was the one clue that might have linked him to the crimes. Instead, the ring linked the crimes to someone else. Chris succeeded in covering up a succession of wicked deeds.

The story line of Match Point shows that in some cases, the harm that results from cover-ups can be secondary to the primary goal of saving face, impression management, and keeping possession of material goods. For Chris, life among the wealthy was so important that he killed his mistress. The murder of the neighbor was a regrettable necessity.

Altruistic Cover-Ups

In testing a theory of BS, left unaddressed will be cover-ups that take the form of altruistic lies, or fibs that people tell when the consequences are trivial. As research shows, human beings lie in a large portion of their interactions. Prevarication is a particularly prevalent form of lying.

Consider the couple who received an invitation to the wedding and reception of a distant relative in a small town hundreds of miles away. Had the events been closer, they might have considered going. While strategizing about how to respond, they hit upon a prevarication. They wrote their regrets, stating they could not go to the wedding because it was on the same day as the farewell reception for an executive in the company for which one of them worked. Neither intended to go to the executive's reception, but they did not mention this.

Thus, through a message that could have more than one meaning, they got themselves off the hook of having to state the bare truth that they did not want to go to the wedding or the wedding reception, which the relatives might have construed as unkind and thus hurtful.

Serial Cover-Ups

Sometimes enactors use a series of cover-ups to distance themselves from their unkind deeds. Floyd Landis defended his 2006 Tour de France victory in many different ways. If illegal drugs were factors in his win, then his defense was a series of cover-ups. He hired expensive lawyers who helped mount a public relations campaign. They also attacked the credibility of the procedures used in testing Floyd's urine for drugs. Floyd wrote a book in his own defense, appeared repeatedly in the print media, and created a website that included a PowerPoint presentation that made a case for his innocence. Despite all of this, Floyd lost his title and his reputation. Many believed he was innocent. He had the support of other world-class bicyclists, medical doctors, and countless sports fans. The banned substance in his urine was strong evidence that he had cheated.

Even his attorneys, who were by any standards of the Clever Fox variety, were unable to save him from the consequences of his alleged use of banned substances. Sometimes, then, cover-ups do not work, even when they cost two million dollars, which is what Floyd had spent by September 2007 when the biking commission stripped him of his title.

Automatic Activation of Cover-Ups

Some enactors have advanced capacities for cover-up based upon years of practice. Their cover-ups arise spontaneously and can be quite elegant. Upon hearing, "What do you want? A harem?" Nick did not skip a beat. His instant response meant he has well-developed brain circuits that automatically activate themselves to form witty, dismissive, distracting cover-ups. Both Vice President Cheney and President Bush appear skilled in truthiness, using phrases such as "We can't cut and run" and "We're doing this for the good of the American people" with such skill that they convince others of their wisdom.

RECIPIENT BUY-IN

The fourth condition of attaining the status of shit is recipient buy-in to cover-ups. As research on lying shows, recipients are more likely to believe the deceptions of persons they trust than the lies of strangers. Ironically, individuals are also more likely to lie to persons with whom they are close. What's more, recipients, especially those in intimate relationships, may have little conscious control over their reactions to cover-ups. In close relationships, recipients want to believe what their loved ones say, and their loved ones know which buttons to push. It is easy to cover-up when recipients are trusting.

Predisposition to Believe Others

In casual or business relationships, cover-ups can still work if persons are predisposed to believe what others tell them and if enactors discover the right buttons to push. For example, a productive worker might ask the boss why she did not get a bonus and others did. The boss could point out something the worker had not done well and overlook her multiple accomplishments. The worker would feel a stab to the heart that signals the activation of "hot" schemas. She would buy in to the boss's view of her work and slink away feeling like shit. Pointing out a flaw in an otherwise exemplary record is a harsh and effective tactic. Enactors who use this ploy are likely to get themselves off the hook and succeed at being shits.

Likewise, citizens are predisposed to believe the words of governors, presidents, and others elected to political office if the politicians have charm and grace and use code words that evoke powerful images. With these tactics, a sizeable portion of their constituency is likely to buy in. The phase "cut and run" is an example. No one wants to be labeled a coward, which is what this phrase implies. Citizens throughout the world tolerate their governments' military aggression because they do not want their country to be perceived as cowardly.

SUMMARY

In summary, being a shit is composed of four parts. The *first* is an unkind deed. The *second* is a desire to save face, to evade responsibility and accountability, and to manage impressions. The *third* is the cover-up itself, which are the actions that enactors take to evade responsibility and accountability. These evasions require spotting and pushing the hot buttons of others or otherwise engaging in behaviors that result in deception and distraction. The *fourth* part is recipient buy-in. Buy-in means recipients believe the cover-ups. Buy-in enables enactors to attain the status of shit. Without recipient buy-in, enactors fail at being shits.

PART TWO

TESTING THE THEORY OF BS

Will the theory hold?

I will now test the theory of BS on a series of cases. These cases are stories of everyday life that I took from novels, newspaper feature news articles, essays, comic strips, and my observations of everyday life. Situations covered are scenarios in family and community life, business, politics, film-making, and the profession of law.

Also included are stories where women as well as men enacted unkind deeds and cover-ups and where both genders were recipients. Finally, the stories span the life course, from childhood to older adulthood. Such variety shows that BS is an equal opportunity status. Will the theory hold? Probably not completely. That's why scientists develop theories—to test them and to change them if there is evidence to do so.

SIX

A SON BORROWS HIS DAD'S CAR

A Thirty-five year-old man, who did not give his name, told a story of borrowing his dad's car for a drive in the country with a woman friend. Deep in a forest, they ran out of fuel. The man walked to a nearby farmhouse where the people there told him he was welcome to their fuel but they could not guarantee how good it was because they had stored it for a while.

The man dumped two or three gallons into the tank, along with a straw he for some reason also used to get the gasoline into the car. The car coughed and started, and the couple arrived at their destination. Taking the advice of a mechanic, the man filled the tank with high octane fuel and two containers of dry gas to compensate for what might have been bad fuel. He also hoped the straw would somehow dissolve.

Back home a few days later, the man's father asked, "How did the car run?" The son said, "Just fine." The father said, "That's funny. It stalls out on me." The son had nothing to say.

Guilt-ridden, the son phoned Click and Clack, the car experts whose radio show Car Talk is syndicated on National Public Radio, and asked them what to do. Either Click or Clack told the son that he had messed up big time. What the son should have done the moment he returned the car was to tell his father that the car ran pretty good but it did stall out a couple of times.

APPLICATION OF THE THEORY

The son committed an unkind deed by putting bad fuel into his dad's car. His motive for covering this up may have been fear of his father's displeasure. His cover-up was withholding information about the bad fuel. The father had no choice but to believe that his son's actions had nothing to do with the car's stalling out.

The advice of the car expert was a pre-emptive cover-up, a kind of CYA (cover your ass). From some points of view, but probably not the father's, it is also humorous, a kind of Clever Fox enactment of BS. Click (or Clack) made this suggestion with lightning speed, which supports the idea that he possesses automatic capacities for activating well-developed schemas related to humor and deviousness. The son, however, lacked these capacities since he had fallen back on a less clever cover-up which was silence, but he may have learned something from Click (or Clack).

Taking a more serious turn, Click and Clack gave the guilt-ridden son their wisdom about whether anything he had done had caused the stalling. The straw was probably not a problem, they said. Their final thought was the fuel injectors might need flushing out. Whether the son suggested this remedy to his dad and came clean about the bad fuel was not part of the radio show.

SEVEN

"It's Easy to Lie to an Honest Guy"

S ome enactors are so good at cover-up that recipients feel as if they are at fault. Lynn Johnston, the author of For Better or for Worse, a daily cartoon syndicated internationally in newspapers, provided an example of this in her depiction of Anthony's responses when his wife Thérèse left him and their young daughter to be with another man.

In her parting words, Thérèse told Anthony that he now had it all, the house and the child, both of which he had wanted. He, therefore, had won. Anthony told a friend, "I feel like such a loser." He said there had been signs of Thérèse's infidelity but he had not suspected a thing. The friend responded, "It's easy to lie to an honest guy."

APPLICATION OF THE THEORY

The friend's words illustrate an important dimension of BS: How easy it is to lie and therefore to cover up when recipients themselves are honest and believe others to be so. Research on lying, as discussed earlier, supports the idea that when recipients trust enactors, lying is facilitated.

Thérèse succeeded in BS of the Clever Fox variety. She committed a series of unkind deeds designed to cover up her affair. Rather than tell Anthony that she had become involved with someone else, she shifted attention from her infidelity to dumping on Anthony, making it seem as if there were something wrong with wanting a child and a home with one's wife.

Anthony responded as Thérèse had hoped. He did not accuse her of anything but instead bought into her construction of reality and experienced himself as a loser. She succeeded at covering up her unkind deeds. With Anthony's help, Thérèse attained the status of shit.

This story also shows a woman enacting unkind behaviors, covering them up, and presumably reaping the rewards of getting her own way and constructing reality in ways that suited her. Although the meanings of the word *shit* are linked to males, women have capacities for unkind deeds and cover-ups as this and other stories show.

This story also shows that enactors may at times strike at recipients' strengths, which, surprisingly, can be hot buttons. For years, Johnston had depicted Anthony as a nice guy, a loving boyfriend and husband, a caring father, and a good provider for his family. Yet, the words of his wife about these qualities made him feel like a loser.

Cover-Up by Swiftboating

Thérèse's cover-up is similar to the strategy of swiftboating, which involves discrediting others by attacking their strong points. As a result of such attacks, high merit is made suspect and even smeared. The term originated during the 2004 U.S. presidential campaign when the Swift Boat Vets and POWS for Truth attacked John Kerry's war record, which was heroic. The last thing Kerry and most other people ever thought was that Kerry could become a coward in the minds of other people. That is exactly what happened. Kerry and his supporters never bought into this depiction, but many other people did.

Swiftboating could be a kind of truthiness because the War Vets and POWS for Truth overlooked Kerry's actual accomplishments. They made up stories that were contrary to the record. That tactic worked because it cast doubt and created impressions. In this instance, the truth no longer was an issue, but perceptions, or truthiness, were.

EIGHT

Sophie and Bill Dump on Each Other

W e now return to Sophie and Bill who were at odds at the opening of this book over the etiquette of teeth brushing. When Bill gagged at the bits of food, spit, and toothpaste Sophie had neglected to rinse from the bathroom sink, he hit one of Sophie's hot buttons that triggered shame and then anger. She struck back. "You're too sensitive." She may have thought she was a Clever Fox because she knew those words would silence him.

They did. She hit a hot button. Bill's reaction was so powerful the muscles in his throat contracted. He was speechless. His mind flooded with memories of other times when friends and family had told him the same thing. It was as if people had called him a sissy his entire life. He thought maybe he was too sensitive, and that was a badge of shame.

Later in the evening, he left his own mouth garbage in the bathroom sink. He, too, thought he was a Clever Fox for his indirect way of getting back at Sophie. When Sophie saw Bill's mess in the sink, she remembered the other times she felt other people had dumped on her. She decided to punish Bill for picking on her. She would not to speak to him for the rest of the night and maybe even into the next day. Who does he think he is? What a shit.

"You asked for it"

Bill noticed Sophie's silence, which hit yet another of his hot buttons. He said, "You asked for it. You dissed me." Sophie felt a familiar stab of shame and remained silent. She thought Bill could be right. Bill felt smug at getting back at her once again, but he was also wounded that she would not speak to him.

APPLICATION OF THE THEORY

Sophie and Bill viewed themselves as Clever Foxes. They enjoyed pressing each other's hot buttons and seeing the reactions. From another point of view, however, they were Reactors. Their responses were instant, but the brain circuits that got activated apparently did not reach the neocortex, the seat of reasoning. Nothing else can explain the short-sightedness of not thinking through the consequences of their unkind deeds and cover-ups. Their cingulate gyrus, where schemas with capacities for empathy are stored, must have been underactive. They did not care that they hurt each other. They were at a standstill and saw no other viewpoints but their own.

It was as if they were in a boxing match. Round one began with the initial unkind deed, which was Sophie's act of leaving mouth rubbish in the sink, Bill's objections, Sophie's cover-up, and Bill's buy-in. Round two was Bill's act of not rinsing away his own mouth leavings, Sophie's silent objections, Bill's cover-up of "You asked for it," and Sophie's buy-in.

Sophie and Bill enacted a common couple scenario. They knew each other's hot buttons and pressed them. By doing this, they shifted attention away from their own wrongdoing and probably got a little rush out of setting each other off.

Both succeeded at being shits because each bought into the other's cover-ups. Their strategies of face-saving, revenge, and punishment could become part of long-term conflict in their marriage. They restore harmony by saying, "I'm sorry. I've been a shit. I love you. Let's kiss and make up."

NINE

Early Successes:
"Stick Your Head in, You Clam"

I n their cleverness and wit, some children have advanced capacities for putting one over on others. Such scenarios can be funny from some points of view and hurtful from others. This story of early successes took place in a coastal town in New England where soft-shelled, long-necked clams are a staple. At the touch of a finger on the head of a live clam, the crustacean pulls its neck and head into its shell.

Twelve year-old Brad, tall, skinny, with a prominent Adam's apple, called eight year-old Marvin "liver-lips," "four-eyes," and "fag." A stricken look flashed onto Marvin's face, replaced instantly with a brave smile. Brad said, "You walk like a girl" and he minced down the sidewalk as he flapped the wrist of his left hand and blew kisses into the air. "You're a fem."

The audience of other children laughed, although a few silent ones felt sorry for Marvin. Marvin struggled not to cry, but tears rolled down his cheeks. As he wiped them away, Brad yelled, "What a sissy." The other children laughed again, though not all.

Marvin ran into his house. A minute later, Margaret, Marvin's mother, leaned out the window and yelled, "Leave Marvin alone." Brad shouted back, "Stick your head in, you clam." Brad laughed and so did the other children, with a few silent once more. Margaret pulled her head back into the house and shut the window. Marvin stayed in for the rest of the day. Margaret did not inform Brad's parents of Brad's conduct.

APPLICATION OF THE THEORY

Brad met all four standards of BS: commission of unkind deeds, refusal to be accountable, cover-up, and recipient buy-in. Brad's initial unkind deed was his mockery of Marvin. When Marvin cried, Brad called him a sissy, a harsh word that blamed the victim and that covered up his role in Marvin's distress. Marvin ran home and told his mother. In defense of her son, Margaret ordered Brad to cut it out.

Brad refused accountability for his behaviors and uttered yet another harsh cover-up when he called Margaret a clam. This name-calling appeared to have resulted in recipient buy-in because Margaret pulled her head in and did not tell Brad's parents of his unkind deeds and harsh cover-ups.

Recipient Cooperation

Both Marvin and Margaret appeared to have cooperated with Brad's cover-ups of his unkind deeds. Rather than apologize when Marvin cried, Brad increased the name-calling. When Margaret objected, Brad called her a name. By withdrawing from the scene, mother and son gave the impression that Brad had succeeded at unkind deeds and cover-ups through blaming the victims.

Marvin might have believed himself to be a sissy and a fem. Margaret might have felt inadequate as a person and a mother. If so, Brad's words were direct hits at these vulnerabilities. Unchallenged, Brad succeeded at BS.

Delight

Brad probably experienced delight, akin to Ekman's notion of duping delight. What's more, the desire to delight himself and his audience may have been a prime motivator. As is often the case in similar situations, some members of his audience empathized with Marvin and Margaret and were confused that anyone would behave as Brad did and that other people would be amused. Still, the children who were unamused also had no idea how to respond.

Classification of Brad's Behavior

How to classify Brad's behavior is challenging. Possibly his conduct was a mixture of Reactor, True Believer, and Clever Fox. That he enjoyed skunking boy and mother suggests that he had disconnected from the hurt he caused. If someone had asked, Brad might not have been able to explain why he behaved as he did, nor would his audience, beyond saying they were having a good time, only kidding around, and meant no harm.

Marvin and his mother may have been collateral damage, where their well-being was secondary to "fun," to the enhancement of Brad's status, and to the gratification that Brad may have felt to have such power over others.

In these behaviors, Brad was a Reactor. Not only would he have been unable to explain why he acted as he did, but he also appeared to have been out of touch with the consequences of his behaviors. However, it is not possible to rule out Brad as a True Believer, one of those who are convinced that what they do is justified and self-evident.

Had adults insisted that Brad and members of his audience explain what was going on in their heads when they amused themselves through hurting Marvin and Margaret, they might have concocted a string of reasons why they did what they did, or they might have clammed up.

There was a bit of elegance to Brad's yell, "Stick you head in, you clam." This could be sufficient to raise his status to Clever Fox. The laughter of his audience showed instant recognition of how clever he was in the depiction of Margaret as a soft-shelled, long-necked crustacean and possibly how relieved they were that Brad had not picked on them.

TEN

Cover-Ups in the Coal Mining Industry

B lame-shifting in the business world is illustrated in *Lost Mountain*, a book about strip coal mining in eastern Kentucky. Author Erik Reece talked to residents of areas near the mining sites about the responses of governmental and mining officials to concerns about the damage done when companies remove tops of mountains to get at the coal beneath.

Owners of trailers that had begun to tilt were told they have old trailers. When a blast damaged the roof of a church, the response was the roof was old. The blame-shifting and evasion of responsibility were put in motion after the companies spent a great deal of money on lawyers to engineer the most effective ways to continue the mining operations while adhering to the letter of the law.

APPLICATION OF THE THEORY

In this case, the unkind deed was property damage and the desire to cover up may have been motivated by money and impression management. The cover-ups involved deflecting blame to the poor condition of the affected property, and the recipients were property owners, who could have been collateral damage because the mine owners' primary motive was profit.

There is no evidence that the recipients of the unkind deeds and cover-ups agreed that the church and their homes were already damaged. Therefore, recipient buy-in appears to be absent. As a result, the mine owners and government officials failed at being shits. Both the deeds and cover-ups were harmful and hurtful. Hurt, however, is not the same as buy-in. The preliminary theory says that recipient buy-in is the standard that enactors must meet in order to succeed at being shits.

A Name for Those who Fail at Being Shits

Here we have run into a situation that the preliminary theory did not anticipate, and that is what to call enactors who fail at being shits. Earlier, I considered and discarded *prick, schmuck*, and *weasel* as possible terms to use to describe those who succeed a being shits. As a result of the failure of the coal mine owners and governmental officials to persuade property owners that their cover-ups were true, I am now re-thinking their possible place in a theory of BS.

The word *weasel* does not work for the coal mine owners and governmental officials because they were not trying to wiggle out of responsibility. They pushed back hard, arguing that the buildings were in poor condition. Even the words *schmuck* and *prick* appear too mild for the degree of callous, self-centered disregard that the mine owners showed.

The word *bastard* might fit. Persons who earn the title *bastard* show a disregard for the impact of their unkind deeds and cover-ups on others. They consider themselves entitled to behave as they do and also to cover up their deeds in any way that gets them what they want. It is a big me and little you kind of thing. I count, and you do not count.

Often those who earn the status of bastard have more power than recipients, as did the governmental officials and mine owners. When recipients consider enactors to be bastards, it shows that recipients have caught onto their unkind deeds and cover-ups. Bastards are persons who commit particularly harsh deeds and cover-ups and who fail at being shits because recipients do not buy into their cover-ups.

Some people may believe that being a bastard is worse than BS. This is so in some circumstances, but the major difference between the two statuses is recipient awareness of what is going on. When enactors have behaved as bastards, recipients know it. When enactors succeed at being shits, recipients do not know it. What's more, the actions of bastards are consistently harsh. The actions of shits range from soft to harsh.

Further testing of the theory on other stories will provide evidence as to whether to accept or reject the inclusion of these other terms in the theory of BS.

Wannabe Clever Foxes

The coalmine owners and governmental officials were not True Believers because they must have known the truth and chose not to admit it. On the other hand, they may have been so intent upon what they wanted that they had talked themselves into believing their own explanations. That would make them True Believers, which is possible though unlikely.

Their actions could also be those of Clever Foxes because of the thought that went into the blame-shifting and also because officials knew what they were doing. Despite the forethought, however, enactors were not clever enough to fool recipients. They failed at being Clever Foxes, and they probably were not True Believers. Perhaps they could be called wannabe Clever Foxes.

ELEVEN

Actions and Not Words as Cover-Ups in the Business World

I n the book, *The Moral Compass of the American Lawyer*, authors Richard Zitrin and Carol M. Langford tell the story of a lawyer named Laura who made it impossible for the plaintiff Sabrina to go forward with a court case. Sabrina had worked in a nursing home, saw unsanitary condition, and brought these conditions to the attention of her boss who fired her, effective immediately. A security guard escorted Sabrina off the premises.

Sabrina hired a lawyer and sued the nursing home for wrongful discharge. Unemployed and a single mother of two, Sabrina moved in with a sister, who lived eighty miles from the city where the suit was to be tried.

The nursing home executives hired Laura who developed strategies to save them from a costly lawsuit and the bad publicity that would result. To do so, Laura arranged for Sabrina to give her deposition at a satellite office of the law firm located on the far side of the city, requiring Sabrina to take a train and two buses to get there.

The main office was in the city center, which would have required Sabrina only to take a train. Sabrina phoned Laura to request that the deposition be taken in the main office. Laura refused, with full knowledge of the burden she had placed on Sabrina.

W hen Sabrina did not arrive for the deposition within ten minutes of the appointed time, Laura noted on the official record that Sabrina did not appear. Laura then filed a motion to dismiss the suit.

In the meantime, Sabrina's lawyer had taken a job in another location, and Sabrina was without counsel. Sabrina phoned Laura to request more time to reply to the motion and to find another attorney. Laura declined both requests.

Back in court to present the facts of the case, Laura persuaded the judge to dismiss the suit. Left unstated in *The Moral Compass* is whether Laura informed the judge of her actions to thwart Sabrina's pursuit of her case, but it is a good guess that Laura was silent on that matter. Her silence can be considered a cover-up.

APPLICATION OF THE THEORY

The story is also silent about Sabrina's response, but we can assume that she was frustrated, hurt, and perhaps even self-blaming. If Sabrina thought she was at fault in any way, then this is another example of the successful enactment of BS: 1) unkind deeds on Laura's part, 2) money and face-saving as motivations not to admit the unkind deed, 3) cover-up through Laura's holding back from the judge how she thwarted Sabrina's attempt to follow through on her suit, and 4) Sabrina's possible response of self-blame.

If Sabrina did not see herself as at fault, then Laura and those who employed her did not achieve the status of being shits, but instead were something else. As in the coal mine story, the term *bastard* comes to mind.

Recipients can be hurt by enactors' behaviors, as Sabrina must have been, but if they see the callousness and entitlement that are behind unkind deeds and cover-ups, then enactors might merely have achieved the status of bastards.

TWELVE

Commentary on What to Call Enactors Who Fail at Being Shits

T he story of Sabrina and Laura is the second instance of enactors' failures at being shits. The first is cover-ups in the coal mining industry. These failures call attention to a need to find a name for those who fail at being shits. The term *bastard* fits enactors whose cover-ups are particularly harsh. Their unkind deeds could be harsh as well. They do whatever it takes to get want they want and to hold on to it regardless of the consequences for recipients.

Those whose deeds and cover-ups are harsh apparently believe they are entitled to act as they do. Their sense of entitlement prevents them from caring about the well-being of others, or, if they experience flashes of care, they dismiss them for the sake of keeping their gains, as Chris did when one of his murder victims appeared to him in a hallucinatory episode. Such enactors lack what Alexander McCall Smith calls moral imagination. It could be that the well-being of others does not exist for them because they do not perceive it, or when they do perceive moral issues, they are secondary to what they want.

Names for Milder Forms of Cover-Up

Milder kinds of cover-up could earn the status of prick, schmuck, and weasel. Like bastards, these individuals also fail at being shits, but their cover-ups and perhaps their deeds are less callous and harmful than those of bastards.

The unkind deeds and cover-ups of pricks, as discussed earlier, may be temporary and a reaction to wounded pride. Recipients may have no idea why enactors' pride is hurt in the first place because the insults are in the mind of enactors only. This was true of William the hero of Notting Hill, discussed previously.

Schmucks are jerks, those whose unkind deeds and cover-ups are uncouth, foolish, and often ridiculous. They may scream accusations and recriminations in order to avoid taking responsibility for their behaviors, but recipients see that they are only covering up.

Weasels may grovel or whine to avoid admitting what they did and to wiggle out of consequences. Again, as in the other failed states, when individuals achieve the status of weasel, recipients have no buy-in.

It is possible that the lesser statuses could also come in three varieties of Reactor, True Believer, and Clever Fox. Logically, this makes sense. Further testing of the theory will show whether there is evidence for this conjecture.

Recipients of unkind deeds and cover-ups are in powerful positions because of their roles in determining whether or not enactors attain the status of shits. Enactors determine everything else; that is, whether they are bastards, pricks, schmucks, or weasels and whether they are Reactors, True Believers, or Clever Foxes.

F igure 1 shows how these statuses may relate to each other. The figure has a diamond shape that symbolizes a hierarchy, with BS at the top. This status is the least common and the highest achievement. Next comes bastard, which is lower than shit in the hierarchy. Following bastard are the statuses of prick, schmuck, and weasel, respectively.

At this point, Figure 1 is hypothetical, an addition to the preliminary theory. The application of the theory of BS to subsequent stories will show whether the addition of these terms for the lower statuses contributes to a more full theory.

Figure 1: A Status Hierarchy of Types of Enactors

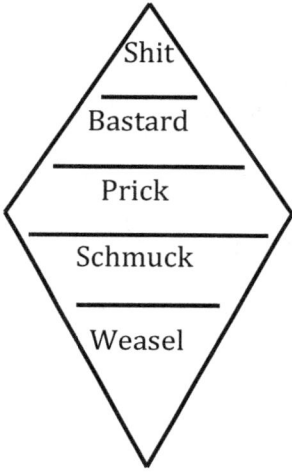

Note: The size of the space allocated to each status suggests the proportions of persons who commit unkind deeds and covers and who achieve the various statuses. At the pinnacle is BS, which has the most status in this hierarchy and is the least common.

THIRTEEN

Drama in the Scottish Highlands:
A True Believer, a Schmuck, or Both?

The story of Jamie in M.C. Beaton's novel *Death of a Scriptwriter*, which took place in the Scottish Highlands, could help to clarify what to call individuals who fail at being shits. Jamie, the scriptwriter of the title, worked earlier in his life as a writing instructor to supplement his then meager income. In this job, he encountered Stuart, a student who had written a television script called Football Fever that Jamie recognized as brilliant but that he told Stuart was rubbish. Stuart died soon after.

When Jamie learned of Stuart's death, he submitted Stuart's script as his own to the BBC, which produced and televised it. The show received great acclaim, and Jamie achieved fame, fortune, and opportunities to write other scripts and to direct films for television.

Jamie's false representation of himself as a talented scriptwriter began to unravel when Angus, Stuart's heir, showed up on a television set where Jamie was in charge to confront Jamie with the theft of Stuart's script. Jamie went off in an explosion of words. He began with an indignant "How dare you?" followed up with a declaration that the script was his and "no one else's" and that he had wasted his time and talent on those students because they were "a bunch of losers" and "no-hopers and wannabes." He exclaimed that he remembered Stuart as a "useless wee faggot."

Angus Punches Jamie

These words must have struck some of Angus's hot buttons because he punched Jamie in the nose. In reaction, Jamie howled "Get the police." The officer who showed up was Hamish MacBeth, the hero of Beaton's novel. Jamie roared at Hamish, "I'm charging this bastard with assault." Hamish ignored Jamie and asked Angus how he had come to the conclusion that Jamie had stolen the script. Jamie interrupted with "Charge him." Jamie shows how persistent enactors can be.

Hamish once again ignored Jamie and coolly prioritized the tasks before him, setting the matter of ownership of the script on top of the list and relegating Angus's physical assault of Jamie as secondary. Hamish announced that he planned to contact the Glasgow police and ask them to investigate who authored the script.

Jamie Apologizes

Upon hearing this, Jamie apologized for calling Stuart a faggot. Next, he said that court appearances can be lengthy and go nowhere, an excellent reason to drop the matter. Finally, he played the work card; that is, deeply held beliefs about the value of work. Work, he implied, was more important than any silly dispute over authorship.

Hamish did not respond. Another character, Fiona, whom Jamie had treated unfairly earlier in the novel by getting her fired on bogus charges, joined the conversation. She said, "I think the matter should be investigated" and noted that "Plagiarism is a serious business." Jamie responded with, "You bitch, you've got it in for me because you're out of a job." Ironically, Jamie had caused Fiona to be fired in the first place. In response to this name-calling and disparagement, Fiona said nothing.

Angus put himself back into the fray and told Jamie that having met him, he cannot believe that Jamie had written a screen play as witty and intelligent as Football Fever. "You're a dead man," he said. That was the end of the scene.

APPLICATION OF THE THEORY

Jamie committed so many unkind deeds it is hard to sort them out. What's more, it is hard to decide which actions are unkind deeds and which are cover-ups. Clearly, stealing the script was an unkind deed, as was telling Stuart his script was rubbish and getting Fiona fired. Calling Fiona a bitch, Angus a bastard, and Stuart a "useless wee faggot" was unkind, but these names also served as attempted cover-ups of Jamie's unkind deeds.

Motivation for Cover-Up

Jamie had a lot to lose if Angus proved he had stolen Stuart's script. Jamie had become a famous man, positioned for even greater fame and fortune. He was at risk for national disgrace and never again to find work as a writer or director, facing years of ignominy and poverty.

Cover-Up

As his treachery was about to be revealed, Jamie let loose with a string of cover-ups that included an indignant "How dare you?" as well as declarations about his own talent and the value of the time he had wasted on those students. He resorted to name-calling, not only of his students but also of Stuart. In response to Angus's punch, he called Angus a bastard. With Fiona, Jamie activated the time-tested tactic of calling her a bitch, a word that humiliates and silences women, laden as it is with woman-hating meanings that have a long history in English-speaking cultures and many other cultures worldwide.

Buy-In

No one had buy-in. Despite his loud and persistent inflammatory language, there is little doubt that anyone took Jamie seriously. Hamish kept his cool and in so doing showed the higher order capacities that Ekman attributed to skilled liars. Hamish's balanced responses to Jamie's forceful words suggest that those who resist the maneuvers of enactors must have skills superior to those of the persons who are attempting cover-up. Beaton depicted both Angus and Fiona as disgusted with Jamie, and they too did not buy into Jamie's constructions of reality, although both of them were less cool in their responses.

Jamie's Status

The recipients of Jamie's cover-ups caused him to fail at BS and thus engineered the downgrading of his status. He earned the title *bastard* when he told Stuart his script was rubbish, stole the script, and then called Stuart names. That is harsh and callous. Likewise, causing Fiona to be fired, disparaging her unemployed status, and then calling her a bitch all fit the definition of bastard. Ironically, Jamie called Angus a bastard when he himself had earned that title. He appeared foolish, like a schmuck, when he yelled, "How dare you?" and uttered his many other transparent cover-ups. When he realized the jig was up, he moved into weasel mode, apologizing, playing the work card, and minimizing the significance of what he had done.

Jamie's story provides additional evidence that giving names to those who fail at BS is warranted. What's more, this story shows that enactors can go into freefall from bastard, to prick, and to schmuck after success at BS. Before Angus found him out, Jamie may have believed that he was a Clever Fox for claiming Stuart's script as his own. He may have been a True Believer in the sense that he convinced himself that he was talented and worthy of the acclaim he received. In the scene under discussion, Jamie could at times to have been in Reactor mode, striking out without thinking in his desperation.

Jamie would have succeeded at BS if any of the recipients had been appeasers; that is, persons who cannot tolerate discord and who do not hold enactors accountable for the sake of peace. Unlike the research findings that DePaulo and associates reported, Jamie did not confess his guilt and seek forgiveness.

Cover-Ups and Dysregulation

The flood of words that Jamie unleashed suggests that he may have experienced dysregulation, meaning that being confronted about his theft of the script might have pushed hot buttons that resulted in his own distress and irrational thinking. His behaviors opens the possibility that enactors of unkind deeds and cover-ups are susceptible to dysregulation.

He might have also intended to distract his accusers by triggering their hot buttons. When enactors succeed at this, then they are off the hook because recipients are too distracted with their own emotios to be able to keep a focus on enactors' behaviors.

Within hours after his vigorous self-defense, Jamie was found murdered on a remote part of the Highlands, his eyes pecked out by vultures. Angus's final words that Jamie was a dead man foretold Jamie's future. Few who enact cover-ups share Jamie's fate, but typically live on, self-satisfied.

FOURTEEN

Dick Cheney Shoots Lawyer
While Others Cover Up

S ometimes enactors of unkind deeds remain silent while others cover up for them. In response to great pressure, they eventually make gestures toward accountability. This was the situation after Vice President Dick Cheney shot Texas attorney Harry Whittington on a 50,000 acre South Texas ranch late on a Saturday afternoon in February 2006.

Briefly, the story goes as follows. On a quail hunt, Harry had a spectacular shot: he killed two birds with two shots. The birds hit the ground in back of the hunting party. As Harry went to retrieve them, Dick heard the beating of wings as a covey of quail burst up from the grass behind him. Harry may have flushed them. Dick wheeled around and fired.

Harry was between Dick and the quail. Birdshot hit Harry in the face, neck, arm, and chest. A few days later, a pellet migrated to Harry's heart, and he had a heart attack.

An International Uproar

The incident produced an international uproar. That a U.S. vice president would shoot somebody is big news in itself, but the responses of the vice president were even bigger news.

Rather than follow the usual procedure of immediately putting out a news bulletin and holding a press conference, there was no public announcement until the next day. What's more, the vice president asked Katherine Armstrong, the ranch owner's daughter, to report the incident. She contacted a reporter at the *Corpus Christi Caller-Times*, the locally published paper. A few hours later, the editors had the story posted on the paper's website where it was picked up and spread around the world.

Cover-ups by Proxy

In a phone interview later that day, Katherine, who was a member of the hunting party, provided details about the shooting. "This all happened pretty quickly," she said. Harry "did not announce — which would be protocol — 'Hey, it's me, I'm coming up.'" She continued, "He didn't do what he was supposed to do. So when a bird flushed and the vice president swung in to shoot it, Whittington was where the bird was."

Katherine further explained that Harry was "peppered" with "little bitty pellets," and no bullets were involved. Indeed, she noted that on another occasion she herself had been peppered with pellets when hunting. Furthermore, the blast had merely broken Harry's skin and "knocked him silly, but he was fine," talking with his eyes open immediately after being shot. By the next day, she said, Harry was "sitting up in bed, yakking and cracking jokes."

She praised Dick at length for the concern he showed Harry, rushing to his aid, directing his medical team to care for Harry, and monitoring Harry's condition at the hospital. Unknown is what Katherine thought after Harry's heart attack.

Dick left Texas the day after the shooting, but not before he visited Harry in the hospital. One of the vice president's spokespersons said that Dick "was pleased" that Harry was "doing fine and in good spirits." She also explained that Katherine made the announcement because "we deferred to the Armstrongs regarding what had taken place at their ranch," adding that no one broke the news to the press earlier because attention, including Dick's, was focused on Harry's well-being. Another spokesperson said that Dick "felt badly, obviously," and he had not been reckless and had not violated any rules. In fact, Dick had not done "anything he wasn't supposed to do."

The Vice President Speaks

After four days of relentless public demand, Dick made his first public statement. He gave an exclusive interview to Brit Hume of Fox News. He said he and no one else pulled the trigger, that it was not Harry's fault, and no one else was to blame. Dick stated that he would never be able to erase from his mind the image of Harry falling. "It was, I'd have to say, one of the worst days of my life, at that moment." He noted that he did not know if he had shot the bird he had aimed for. His concern was for Harry.

He responded to the rumor that the reason for the delay in reporting was because he was drunk and he wanted time for the alcohol to clear from his body. He said he had had one beer at lunch. "Nobody was drinking. Nobody was under the influence."

Altruistic Motives for the Delay

Dick attributed the delay in the public announcement to his desire to have accurate information about Harry's condition before informing the media, and he also wanted Harry's children to be informed privately, before the story made its way to the public, he explained. Harry's wife knew because she had been at the ranch at the time of the shooting.

Dick defended Katherine Armstrong as the initial spokesperson because she was an eyewitness. Brit Hume observed that having Katherine make the announcement to a local newspaper gave the impression that this strategy was an attempt to minimize the story and have it appear "as a little hunting accident." Dick said this was not so, and he repeated that accuracy was foremost in his mind.

As shown earlier, when Harry left the hospital after six days, he expressed concern for the vice president and the vice president's family and minimized his own and his family's suffering. He left uncorrected the impression that he, Harry, had had broken the rules of hunting and the vice president had done nothing wrong.

What is striking about this story is what no one said. For instance, neither Dick in his interview with Brit Hume nor any of his spokespersons corrected the impression given during the first few days after the shooting that Harry alone had been at fault and that Dick had done nothing wrong. In actuality, for hunting of any kind, the rules are to see your target before you shoot, to make sure you know where each member of your party is before you shoot, and to never sweep around without knowing who or what is in your line of fire.

In bird hunting, the rule is not to fire until you can see the sky between the earth and the bird and not until the silhouette of the target is against the sky. Further details about the rules of hunting are posted on many websites including that of the Texas Parks and Wildlife Department (TPWD) that publish the Ten Commandments of Shooting Safety.

A comparison of Dick's actions with the Ten Commandments shows that Dick broke two of the commandments: 1) "Be sure of your target and what is in front of and beyond your target" (number 3) and 2) "Know your safe zone-of-fire and stick to it" (number 6), which command includes the injunctions to "Be sure you know where your companions are at all times. Never swing your gun or bow out of your safe zone-of-fire." These are standards of safety that hunters know well.

APPLICATION OF THE THEORY

Application of the preliminary theory of BS will aid in the discovery about whether Dick Cheney's behavior regarding the shooting of Harry Whittington was an enactment of BS.

The Unkind Deed

Did Dick do something unkind? Yes. He shot a hunting companion. Everyone knows the first rule of hunting is not to shoot the people you hunt with. Dick thus met the first condition of BS.

Motivation for Cover-Ups

Did he meet the second condition, which is a desire to evade responsibility for this unkind deed? Dick's silence and tardy explanation, in combination with his well-known fondness for secrecy, suggest that he wanted to avoid accountability. He must have been shaken by what he had done, and he also could have wanted to save face and avoid punishment. He may have imagined his enemies laughing at what a fool he was to shoot another hunter. He may have feared that he could be charged with reckless endangerment of human life. Maybe he had a little too much to drink.

His motivation for allowing Katherine and other spokespeople to blame Harry and then not retract their statements appears to be an attempt to minimize the gravity of the incident, a face-saving strategy.

The Cover-Ups

The third condition involves the cover-ups themselves. There were many. First was the withholding of the news. Second was the often-repeated statement that Harry was in the wrong. Third was the assertion that Dick had done what he was supposed to have done. Fourth was the minimization of the size of the pellets and the significance of the shooting itself.

The fifth involved Dick's and his spokesperson's silence regarding the injustice of blaming Harry, even after Dick said the shooting was his fault in the Fox News interview. The sixth was his decision not to retract Katherine's statement that the pellets were "little bitty," indeed giving the impression that this was a "little hunting accident."

Machiavelli's advice to politicians comes to mind here. His advice was to follow up unkind acts with the pretence of contrition, which Dick did. He was effusive in his concern for Harry and Harry's family. He conveniently overlooked facts, such as it was he who had violated two rules of hunting and Harry had not violated any. He did not speak these simple truths. He let stand the initial impression that Harry had broken the rules of hunting and the pellets were tiny.

What's more, the county sheriff's department helped in the cover-up. The sheriff investigated the incident but he chose not to file charges. The law of reckless endangerment did not apply to the vice president. Based on these facts and interpretations, it can be concluded that Dick covered up. He therefore met the third condition of BS, aided by several spokespersons on his payroll and Katherine Armstrong, an experienced hunter herself.

Recipient Buy-In

The final condition to be met involves the actions of recipients. By his silence on who was responsible for shooting him and his effusive concern for Dick's well-being, Harry gave the appearance of acquiescing to the construction of reality that he was at fault and Dick was not. Harry minimized the impact of the shooting on himself and his family. He evaded holding Dick responsible for breaking rules of hunting. Instead, he pointed out that Dick had suffered far more than he, Harry, had.

Harry's silence, evasion, and acquiescence met the fourth condition of BS. Harry may have acted out of altruistic motives of not wanting to cause more problems, but he may also be a man of deep empathy and self-sacrifice, perhaps to a fault. Some commentators believed that the president's or vice president's office had directed Harry's statement. Whatever Harry might have thought privately is unknown.

Had Harry declared that Dick had broken rules, then Dick would only have met the conditions of being a bastard. Dick might also have met the conditions of being a weasel because he prompted spokespersons and maybe even Harry to construct reality in ways that enabled him to wiggle out of responsibility. By his apparent complicity, Harry missed an opportunity to hold the vice president accountable.

Dick's Classification

Whether Dick is a Reactor, a True Believer, or a Clever Fox is also open to interpretation. Some may judge him to be a True Believer, in that he is convinced that his words and actions were based on concern for Harry's well-being.

Whether by design or accident, Dick was clever not to rescind the initial statements that Harry broke the rules of hunting and he had not. His global statement of responsibility did not erase these initial impressions. Such statements muddy accountability and may also create truthiness. Finally, some may believe that Dick acted as a bastard whether or not Harry really felt sorry for the vice president.

FIFTEEN

The Case of the Missing Coffee Grinder

I n a Modern Love feature in the Lifestyle section of the Sunday *New York Times*, Heather Fenby, a performing artist in Manhattan, described a mutually brilliant *pas de deux* with her boyfriend, whom she did not name, over a missing coffee bean grinder. The events began when the boyfriend's house burned down, and Heather took him into her two hundred and fifty square foot Manhattan flat.

The boyfriend filled the place with clutter, some of which he lifted off the sidewalks of New York. He also moved, hid, and even took some of Heather's stuff, including her coffee grinder. When she asked him if he had seen the coffee grinder, he said he had not. She said he must have moved it because she had not. He said it was no wonder you can't find anything. Look at this place.

Cover-Ups and Hot Buttons

Apparently this struck a hot button. Heather wailed, "I want my life back the way it was." The boyfriend responded, "There is no way back. Time is a construct." Heather resisted this deflection and demanded that he "stop bringing more stuff in the house." He came back with, "Who moved my cheese?" in "a squeaky, panicky voice." Heather wrote, "Creepiest of all was his wide-eyed stare of infinite Buddhist compassion."

Heather then reflected upon her expectations of their life together, when, based on the boyfriend's "stratospheric IQ," she had anticipated "nonstop witty repartee and transcendent intimacy." Instead, she noted that he had put his intelligence "in the service of deflection and obfuscation." With these words,

Heather named his strategies and thus appeared to have succeeded in resisting his cover-ups.

So far, the boyfriend had made several brilliant moves, and Heather had resisted them all. Their *pas de deux* cannot be classified as the full flowering of BS because Heather refused to comply with the boyfriend's intimations that she was at fault. Even so, the dance continued.

Name-Calling and Trouncing Away

After Heather "took the apartment apart" for two days in a vain search for the coffee grinder, another conflict erupted, which ended when the boyfriend trounced out of the flat, declaring that he would have helped Heather find the grinder but she was acting too "nutty." Heather sobbed and wailed. Then she resolved to make her way out of her confusion by "furtively" consulting books on abusive relationships. She discovered she was at fault, "abusive and controlling" with a "hair-trigger temper, who shouted and threw things, who nagged, bullied and belittled."

Despite her belief that she was at fault, Heather persisted in wanting her coffee grinder back. Weeks later, she directly asked him if he had taken it. Actually, she did not ask directly, because they were in bed, he with his back to her. She spoke to the back of his head. In response, the boyfriend said, "perhaps." This did not satisfy her. She inquired a second time and heard "maybe" which she interpreted as a "yes." Hearing this, she asked why he had not simply told her rather than watch her rummage through the flat several times looking for it. He answered, "I knew you'd be mad. And then you were too out of control to talk to." Heather did not say anything for a time. Then she asked him to bring it back. He said, "Sure." Heather did not share her response, but she continued to hope that she would get her coffee grinder back. Months later the appliance remained missing. Heather again inquired as to its whereabouts.

Heather's description of what happened next suggests that she may have had some awareness that he was the hunter and she the prey because she "could tell" she had "walked into a trap" by the slight smile that preceded his response: "It's been back for ages. Not that you'd notice."

The boyfriend then pointed to a shelf just below the ceiling far above Heather's line of vision. The object he pointed to, however, was not her grinder, but a substitute. She told him that. He hooted, "That's just perfect." He said that she had "gone on and on about the thing" and she "wouldn't recognize it if it bit" her. He next informed Heather that she was so focused "on grasping and griping and guarding and hoarding" that she had "no idea what really matters" He ended with, "It's a $15 appliance, Heather."

The Boyfriend Scores

Heather capitulated. She heaped blame upon herself in the form of viewing the substitute grinder as a symbol of her "materialistic, bean-counting, unevolved soul" and gave human attributes to the shelf on which it sat as radiating "an uneasy, reproachful aura." She was so contrite she no longer ground her coffee beans but used pre-ground coffee.

An Alternative Point of View

As often happens when one gives in to persistent characterizations of the self as in the wrong when one is not, an outsider, in this case one of Heather's friends, attempted to show Heather another interpretation of the boyfriend's actions. Heather's friend informed Heather that the boyfriend lied to amuse himself and to avoid admitting that he had taken the coffee grinder. She also said the boyfriend wanted Heather to be disoriented and confused and to mistrust her own good sense. According to the friend, the boyfriend's tactics almost convinced Heather that "black was white."

With this new perspective, the scales appeared to fall from Heather's eyes. She experienced a "melodramatic crystalline epiphany" in which she saw her complicity as a sham where, in her desire to take him at his word, she acted as if she believed him that he had not taken the coffee grinder. The boyfriend found a place to sublet and moved out. Heather's apartment was once more uncluttered, but she found her life uninteresting.

Over time Heather had another epiphany in the form of a conviction that she had been excessively engulfed by a "sense of being rooked." She reasoned that it actually was possible that she "had no idea what really mattered" and that the boyfriend was right. The boyfriend returned to live with Heather. Now Heather and the boyfriend "wrangle" about an Elvis phone that he has tucked behind a wrought iron monstrosity he had dragged off the sidewalk. The phone was out of sight to accommodate her wishes, and the monstrosity somehow had its own song, "one we created together," signifying a new level of peace and harmony.

APPLICATION OF THE THEORY

The boyfriend committed unkind deeds and unkind cover-ups. He took the coffee grinder. Following that was a series of actions that covered up his theft. He brought a grinder into the flat, not Heather's but another. He placed it outside of Heather's line of vision. He did not tell her a grinder was back.

Motivation to Cover Up

The boyfriend did not share his reason for the theft of the grinder and then did not tell Heather he had done so. We are left to guess his motives. Heather's friend could have been right about the boyfriend wanting to have some fun and avoid admitting he had taken the grinder. If so, he enacted Ekman's version of duping delight. He seemed to have enjoyed playing her. Another motive for cover-up could have been he was too lazy to buy a coffee grinder for his office. Not only that, he may have had no control over taking other people's things. In other words, he may have been a kleptomaniac and was too ashamed to admit it. After all, he took things off New York sidewalks. Thus, his cover-ups could have been related to face-saving.

Avoidance of consequences may have been an additional factor. The boyfriend said if he had told Heather he knew she would have been mad. This could account for the multiple cover-ups. Only the boyfriend knows. If avoidance of Heather's anger was his motive, then he was short-sighted because with just a little bit of imagination he would have realized that concealing the truth would make Heather even madder.

Impression management could have been at play as well, with the boyfriend not wanting to appear as if Heather could outfox him. He may have wanted to impress an imaginary audience—or friends he may have had at the corner pub—with his talents for duplicity, hoodwinking, and gaslighting.

Cover-Up

The boyfriend covered up each time Heather asked him if he had taken the grinder. The first was when Heather wanted to know if he had seen it. He said he had not. He may have meant to prevaricate, which he did, in the sense that he had not seen it lately, which could have been a literal answer to the question. In actuality, he knew where it was.

The second was when Heather said he must have moved it because she had not. This time he gaslighted. He had cluttered the flat, but he blamed the mess for not being able to find the coffee grinder.

The third time occurred when Heather tore the place up looking for it, and he left the apartment saying he would have helped her search but she was being nutty. He probably went to the pub to tell his buddies about how he was putting one over on his girlfriend.

The fourth was when Heather and the boyfriend were in bed, and he equivocated with "perhaps" and "maybe" when she asked him directly. She then wondered why he had not told her he had taken it, and he said she "was too out of control to talk to," a perfect blame-the-victim answer. This silenced Heather for a time, a typical response to being not at fault. She eventually was able to speak and asked him to bring it back. He said, "Sure," as if all she ever had to do was ask, yet another blame-the-victim cover-up. He then scolded Heather on how grasping and griping she is and what a trivial matter a missing coffee bean grinder is. He minimized his serial unkind deeds and cover-ups and reduced them to the trivial matter of a $15 appliance.

Buy-In

With this final series of cover-ups Heather had buy-in, and the boyfriend succeeded at BS. Until that time, Heather had resisted most of the boyfriend's cover-ups. She even named some as "deflection and obfuscation," noted the mockery the boyfriend conveyed in words, tone of voice, and body language, and pointed out his name-calling.

The boyfriend persisted and finally struck home when he called Heather nutty and left the flat. In response, Heather consulted research on domestic violence that led her to conclude she was at fault. This signified that she had bought into the boyfriend's cover-ups, with the help of what many would consider outmoded views on domestic abuse. With the buy-in, Heather enabled the boyfriend to be a shit. Unknown to Heather, the sources she consulted were based on outmoded customs and traditions. Mental health professionals today recognize that targets of abusive behaviors often appear angry, frazzled, and confused while perpetrators come across as cool, charming, and well-adjusted.

The boyfriend scored big time when he went on about Heather's griping and hoarding. He minimized what he had done by pointing out that the grinder was only worth fifteen dollars. Heather capitulated and even heaped blame upon herself. The boyfriend was clever enough to convince Heather that she was at fault.

By the end of her story, Heather accommodated to the boyfriend's tastes and found herself amused by the junk he collected. She did not report whether he appropriated any more of her possessions or committed any other unkind deeds and cover-ups. She also did not report whether he ever admitted that he had taken the grinder and then played cat and mouse with her for months. She may have chosen to overlook his lack of accountability.

The act of cluttering up her apartment by itself was not an unkind deed as long as it was okay with Heather. What's more, the boyfriend accommodated Heather by keeping the Elvis phone out of sight. Here at last are small indicators of mutuality and reciprocity between this couple and not unkind deeds and cover-ups. Left unstated is whether the boyfriend mended his ways and Heather realized that he had dumped on her while they were in bed together.

The Boyfriend's Classification

With a few words and minimal body language, the boyfriend showed mastery of the cover-up. Few equal him, not only in the skill with which he delivered cover-ups, but in the depth and breadth of his inventory. He had the skills of a Clever Fox.

Heather resisted for a time and proved to be a good match. During those times, she undermined the boyfriend's efforts at BS Taking the grinder and substituting another were trivial, the actions of a prick or schmuck. Moreover, the boyfriend appeared to have been motivated to gaslight Heather for the sport of it, which too sounds like the actions of a prick or schmuck. Finally, his cover-ups at times were harsh, even bastard quality. Besides gaslighting, he mocked, called Heather names, trounced out, and accused her of hoarding and carping.

In summary, the boyfriend was a master and Heather was a match, but the boyfriend eventually convinced Heather that she was wrong about the coffee grinder. The final scene of their story suggested that Heather had capitulated.

SIXTEEN

Drama in Dublin:
Success and Then Failure at BS

I n some cases recipients eventually see through cover-ups that formerly had worked, and enactors lose their status as shits. Such was the case in *Quentins*, Irish novelist Maeve Binchy's best-seller. For much of the book, the heroine Ella, an unmarried recent college graduate, believed the cover-ups of her older lover, Don, a socially prominent financier who was married and the father of two sons. Don succeeded at BS over a long period of time. When Ella eventually saw Don's actions for what they were, namely cover-ups of unkind deeds, she called him a bastard and dumped him.

Don's earliest achievement of BS occurred during Ella's and Don's first argument that started when Ella expressed indignation that Don had gone to Spain with his wife after he had implied he was going there alone on business.

Ella then asked Don if he still had sex with his wife. He responded with indignation, stating that if she did not believe that he could love her, Ella, and still have sex with his wife, then they didn't have much to talk about, did they? With this response, Don did not answer Ella's question. This is prevarication, a clever cover-up whose meanings can be taken in more than one way.

Ella did not buy into this equivocation, a sign of resistance, and asked again. Don said nothing. Ella said the answer is yes, then. Don told Ella that someone must have hurt her badly if she believed such a thing of him, another attack on Ella that diverted attention from the question that Ella had asked.

Ella said that is not so—no man had hurt her before. She told him not to make her into some kind of freak. Ella here showed admirable resistance to Don's construction of reality, reminiscent of Heather's resistance to her boyfriend's constructions of what happened to the coffee grinder.

Don ignored Ella's request not to distort who she is. He also evaded her questions about whether he still had sex with his wife. Instead, he asked Ella how she knew his wife had been with him in Spain. Ella cooperated with the evasion and answered his question: She had phoned their home and the maid had said the lady of the house was in Spain.

In response, Don got sarcastic. He thanked Ella for being a "spy," for "jumping to conclusions," and for not believing him when he told her he loved her. He made a strong argument for his "utter" honesty with Ella from the start, telling her the score, telling her the truth, meeting her parents, and calling them when she did not answer her phone. He asked and answered his own question: "Are these the actions of some kind of shit? No, I think they're what a man who loves you might do."

Ella Capitulates

Don dumped on Ella for her lack of faith in him while she grew increasingly horrified that she could have mistrusted him. Then he made for the door. She caught him at the garden gate. She cried and begged forgiveness. By this action, Ella capitulated to Don's constructions of reality and enabled him to be a shit.

Ella was involved with Don for more than two years. One day, as she waited for Don for a lunch date at Quentins, which was a restaurant and the main setting for Binchy's novel, she saw a story about Don on the front page of the newspaper. He had absconded to Spain with his investors' money on the early morning flight from Dublin. He had joined his wife and children who were there waiting for him.

Don had looted his investment company of its assets, ruining his many customers, including Ella's parents who had entrusted Don with their life savings. Ella had a terrible time believing that Don would do such a thing and rejected the idea that he would leave her to be with his family. She believed he never would leave without telling her.

Later news reports stated that Don had been in Spain the week before to make arrangements for his move there. Ella was appalled because he had made those arrangements when she was in Spain with him. He had explained his long absences during that trip as necessitated by the press of his business. This is duplicity in action.

Ella clung to her belief that Don loved her for much of the novel, despite his lack of contact, although early on she told her parents that she was angry at herself because she had not found an ordinary person to love but had instead loved a criminal. Ella's mother replied in a perfect rendition of a principle discovered in research on lying, "Everyone trusts people when they love them." Anthony's friend said something similar when Anthony's wife Thérèse left him.

Don Fails at BS

As Ella reflected on what Don had done to his investors, Ella called him a bastard who had conned people out of their money and used it for the unkind deeds of "shoring up a love nest for himself, wife, and kiddies," while she, Ella, waited for him in the hotel swimming pool. Lest readers miss the point, Binchy had Ella use the term *bastard* to characterize Don three times.

Throughout the novel, four other characters also used that term to describe him and his ever-growing list of unkind deeds and cover-ups. The unkind deeds included presenting himself to investors as charming, affable, and trustworthy, stealing their money, ruining them financially, and then setting himself up in another country beyond the reach of Irish law enforcement. He then faked his own death to escape consequences of his fraud, a cover-up taken to the extreme.

As Ella was getting over the hurt that Don had caused, she met and fell in love with a multi-millionaire from the United

States who had roots in Ireland. The two were engaged to be married, with the fiancé putting down roots in Ireland.

Ella was ready for Don in the final scene where he sobbed as Dublin police guards surrounded him. He howled to Ella, "I did it for you, Angel. I did it for you." These statements are cover-ups that Ella did not believe. Don had not defrauded investors for Ella. He had not fled to Spain for her. Don displayed cowardice, a whiny cover-up, and ongoing evasion of responsibility, a classic depiction of a weasel.

In much of the novel, Don showed the ingenuity of a Clever Fox in terms of prevarications, the boldness of his duplicity, and the falseness of his rhetorical question about whether his actions were those of a shit. As evidence of Don's unkind deeds and cover-up accumulated, and, with the support of friends and the love of her fiancé, Ella disentangled herself from Don's constructions of reality. Through her new understandings of Don, she downgraded his status to that of bastard.

Over time, Don's capacities for ingenuity in cover-up diminished. His justifications for what he did were in the mode of Jamie, the failed scriptwriter: whiny, weasely, and unconvincing.

Desire for Apology

Binchy's depiction of the saga of Ella and Don illustrates another important aspect of unkind deeds and cover-ups. Ella longed for an apology. One night, she dreamed that Don had sent her a text message on her mobile phone. It contained only a few words: "Sorry, Angel." The dream did not come true. Don was first a shit, then a bastard, and finally a weasel. He never apologized. He never came clean. He evaded accountability for his unkind deeds and cover-ups to the end.

SEVENTEEN

When a Man Wants Two Women

I now return to the case of Cara and Nick whose story began this investigation. The couple discussed the appropriate size of a harem in a country pub. After Cara let herself be distracted by Nick's statement about two women not being much of a harem, he and Cara had another drink and then went to her house for the night. Although they maintained separate homes, they spent most of their time together at her place.

Within a few days, Cara asked Nick for more information about the other woman. He told Cara that her name was Moira and that Moira knew about Cara.

"How long have you known her?" Cara asked.

"Six weeks." Nick answered.

"What are your plans?"

"She smokes. She is not permanent. Smoking is a deal breaker."

"What does that mean?"

"I'm with you now, aren't I? Where is she?" Nick then reached for Cara and held her in his arms. "I'm a bastard," he said. "I hurt you." Cara put her head on Nick's chest. They were quiet. Cara wondered about the implications of these words, but she did not ask. It was as if her brain had shut down.

The next day, Cara could not concentrate on her work. Her intuition told her that Nick had not told her the whole story. Nick was director of human resources for a large company. Cara searched the company's website for the name *Moira*. The comptroller's name was Moira. She had held the job for ten years. Nick had joined the company twelve years before. Nick had known Moira longer than he had known Cara.

Cara remembered the times Nick had said he went out for drinks "with people at work" and that "people at work" had arranged a surprise birthday lunch for him. One time, when he had a dispute with the board of directors, "a friend from work" had helped straighten things out. He made several business trips over the years with "people at work." Moira had to be the "friend at work" and the "people at work."

N ow that Cara had Moira's full name, Cara did an Internet search and found Moira's property and voting records. Moira was the only voter and the only adult in Moira's home. Two minor children also lived there, Margaret and Megan. At least she is not married, Cara thought.

Cara phoned Nick at work. "I know you've known Moira for years."

"Who told you?" Nick exclaimed.

"I looked it up on the Internet. She lives with her two children and owns her own home."

The line went dead. Cara thought they had been disconnected. She phoned him back.

"Hello," Nick said.

"Hello," Cara said. "We got cut off."

"I don't want to talk." The line went dead. Cara felt as if a truck had run over her. Cara waited a few days to hear from Nick. He did not phone, e-mail, or stop by. She e-mailed him

I'm sorry our relationship has come to this.

Nick wrote back:

What do you expect when you cyberstalk my friends? I would have been happy to answer any questions you have.

With the word "cyberstalker" buzzing in her head, Cara looked the word up in Wikipedia, the on-line encyclopedia. Enlightened, she thought she might not be a cyberstalker, but was unsure. Not yet willing to give up, Cara then sent Nick several questions about what Moira meant to him. He ignored them. She e-mailed to ask him to be a man of his word and answer her questions, which she repeated. He responded

> I'm not answering any more questions. Please do not e-mail me again.

Stung once more, Cara decided to honor Nick's request not to e-mail him again. She held back powerful desires to phone, write, and sit on the stonewall outside his condo and wait for him to come home. She did not do this.

A Large, Pink Birthday Card

Like Ella, Cara hoped for months that Nick would get in touch, say he was sorry, that he loved her, and that he would do anything so that they could be together. He did get in touch. Six months after what she thought was the final e-mail, Nick sent her a large hand-made pink birthday card with hearts and X's and O's on the front and signed "To Cara, Love, Nick" in large letters.

She e-mailed him, asked what the card meant, and said she did not want to read too much into it. She asked him to phone or e-mail so they could talk. She told him she missed him. He e-mailed immediately. This is what he said.

> The card doesn't mean anything. You're a good person. You were good to me. It was right to remember your birthday.

That, as they say, was that. This e-mail struck the blow that severed the tie that linked Cara to Nick. Yet, Nick was not done with Cara. Two months after Nick sent Cara the birthday card, Nick got in touch through e-mail. He began with

I probably should not be doing this but what the hell. I've been playing on Google Earth and tried to bring up your house but without success.

He said he looked for "the circle around the tree" in Cara's garden, confessed that he was "beginning to feel old and mortal" and complained about work. He had done an Internet search to see what Cara had been up to and found information that "suggests you are busy." Left unmentioned was whether he had cyberstalked Cara. Then he asked if Cara had any news.

Cara wrote back a week later. She told him that his e-mail had come at a time when she was missing him especially, and she wondered about psychic connection. She continued

We've had such wonderful times together that I said to myself this week I find it hard to believe that these times were not wonderful for you, too. I cherish my memories of us together and would like the barriers between us to dissolve. I can't see how that is possible, although there was a time when I would have done all I could to have seen that happen. I'm glad you think of me, and I hope you cherish the memories.

She told him a bit of news about a commitment ceremony she had attended the week before. She said that the vows the two women exchanged were words "I wish you and I could have said to each other: 'Loving what we know about each other and trusting what we do not know.'" She continued

My wish for you is that you say those words to someone who is worthy of them. You have a full life with Moira and her family. Unless things change drastically and you finally come clean, I see little hope that I would want even an e-mail friendship with you.

There is far too much unexplained cruelty from you to me for me to ignore. You did say once, 'I hurt you,' and you were contrite. I actually need much more explanation than that.

Nick responded right away.

> OK. I thought we could have had an email correspondence but I read your words 'I cannot see how we can maintain a connection even via e-mail' and I respect them. We did have wonderful times and they keep coming back to me when I least expect them, and yes I also 'cherish' those memories.

He added, "I cannot recall" the cruelty or what it was about. He continued

> Sometimes you cannot explain everything in this world. I hope that will always be the case. We need some 'unknowns' even when it's our own behavior. The world is healthier with some mystery in it, even self mystery.

If Cara needed more reason to conclude a relationship with Nick was hopeless, she had it.

A few months later, U.S. Attorney General Alberto Gonzales testified under oath before a Senate committee that he "cannot recall" the events that led up to the firing of eight U.S. federal attorneys. Subsequent records and testimony of others revealed that he had been completely involved in the firings. President Richard M. Nixon used the faulty memory cover-up during the Watergate scandal in the early 1970s, as mentioned earlier.

Nick is in good company when he invoked the cover-up of not remembering. There must be a school where people learn how to learn to cover-up.

APPLICATION OF THE THEORY

The story of Cara and Nick, like the tales of Ella and Don and of Heather and her boyfriend, is a complex chain of events. Application of the theory will reveal whether Nick met the standards of BS and how Cara might have enabled him to do so.

Nick had committed an unkind deed, which was to date another woman named Moira while he was involved with Cara.

Motivations for Cover-Ups

Nick left unstated his motive for covering up the place of Moira in his life, but he may have had more than one. He may have wanted both women—one for work and one for home. If this is so, Nick is not alone. Don wanted two women. These men stand for countless others. Women, too, are not immune to wanting more than one romantic involvement. The desire to keep one's gains is a typical motivation of cover-up.

There are other possible motivations for Nick's unkind deeds and cover-ups. He may have preferred Moira over Cara but was afraid to tell Cara because he did not want to put up with her reactions, which could have been hurt, anger, and recrimination. In other words, he wanted to avoid consequences. In addition, Moira may have been important to Nick in his career, and he may have valued business success more than his connection to Cara. Only Nick can account for his motivations, although his statement about two women may be the closest to the truth.

Nick's Cover-Ups and Cara's Buy-Ins

Nick engaged in a series of cover-ups. The first was humor when he said, "Two women? That's not much of a harem." Cara bought into that one for a short time, temporarily diffusing a hot situation and enabling Nick to continue his cover-ups.

Nick then declared himself a bastard for hurting Cara. She allowed him to hold her in his arms, leading her to wonder about what these words meant for them as a couple.

The next cover-up was to divert attention from his lie about how long he had known Moira. When Cara told him she knew he had known Moira for years, instead of admitting his lie, he asked, "Who told you?" Cara answered Nick's question instead of insisting that he admit he had lied. Cara once again allowed herself to be distracted from her own agenda. Yet another time, she enabled Nick to succeed at covering up.

Nick then grabbed complete control when he accused Cara of cyberstalking. The word silenced Cara. After checking the meaning of the word in Wikipedia, she thought she probably had not cyberstalked, but she vowed not to search the Internet for any more information about Moira. Once again Nick succeeded at BS. Everything went his way because Cara bought into his version of the situation.

The first time Nick hung up without warning was another cover-up but it had no effect on Cara because she thought they had been disconnected. When she phoned him back, and he said, "I don't want to talk," that was yet another cover-up in the form of evasion. This cover-up devastated Cara. She was hurt and confused. Her view of Nick as a charming, thoughtful man clashed with this version of him. She had her first inkling of how callous Nick could be. Nick was beginning to fail at BS. Subsequent exchanges confirmed this change of status.

Nick's Show of Virtue

Nick had presented a façade of virtue when he told Cara that he would have been glad to answer any questions. Cara took him at his word, but he answered none of them and told her he would not answer any more. When Nick followed up his refusal with a request not to e-mail him, she could hardly bear it, but something changed, too. Still hurt but no longer confused,

Cara began to see Nick's actions as callous and uncaring. In so doing, Cara refused buy-in to Nick's cover-ups.

Cara abided by Nick's request not to e-mail him. She also did not phone him, drop by his office or home, or write to him. She hoped that he would seek to reconnect in honest ways. He did not. The meaningless pink birthday card was the last act of their drama. She was done. To Cara, his final e-mail about the circle around her tree and her response about love and trust were postscripts that went nowhere.

Nick Fails at BS

Nick, like Don in Binchy's novel *Quentins*, succeeded on some counts in BS before Cara came to know him as he was. His harsh cover-ups and refusal to talk things out led her to think of him as a bastard, just as Ella had done at the end of *Quentins.* Ironically, Nick had called himself a bastard. It was only in light of subsequent events that Cara agreed with him. She also thought he might be a weasel in his cowardice in refusing to talk. Nick's talent at cover-up rivals that of Heather's boyfriend. Nick crashed and burned, however, and the boyfriend at the end of Heather's tale was ensconced in the tiny, cluttered flat.

Nick Fails Again

Nick enacted several different cover-ups. He was a Clever Fox for some of them. For others, such as the birthday card that meant nothing, he was clueless, perhaps a Reactor, or possibly a type that does not yet have a name. He was a Reactor when he was firing away with his cover-ups. Nick's thoughts on mystery, "even self-mystery," suggest that he has advanced capacities for being a True Believer as well. These thoughts were an elegant explanation as to why he "cannot recall" his cruelties. By so doing, he excused his own actions. Nick is like many others who commit unkind deeds and then cover up. They are unrepentant and unaccountable. They hold on to their constructions of reality to the end.

EIGHTEEN

Clarence Thomas Markets his Book[1]

U nkind deeds and cover-ups burned through cyberspace in September 2007 when Clarence Thomas revived a controversy that had been dormant for more than twenty-five years. The controversy was whether or not Clarence had sexually harassed Anita Hill when he was head of the Equal Employment Opportunity Commission and she worked under his supervision at the Commission.

Clarence gave the controversy great play in the launching of his autobiography, *My Grandfather's Son*. He granted an interview with Steve Kroft of CBS's 60 Minutes, his first interview since the Senate confirmed him in 1991 as an associate justice of the U.S. Supreme Court. On national television, Clarence described Anita Hill in words that throughout history have silenced women: "touchy" and "sensitive to slights." He also said Anita was a hypocrite in her religious beliefs and that she was so incompetent that she was "let go" from a law firm. In his book, Clarence said Hill was used by left-wing radicals, among many other charges. Clarence said all of this with an ironic smile on his face and in a gentle tone of voice as if everyone knows this about Anita Hill. Machiavelli recommended just this style of delivery.

Anita Refuses Buy-In

Anita responded a few days later in a *New York Times* commentary. She wrote that she refused to let him "reinvent" her. She denied his depiction of herself and presented

---

[1] Valandra contributed to this chapter.

convincing evidence that Clarence's words were untrue. She was not fired from a law firm. She was a professor of law for many years at Oral Roberts University, which is a conservative Christian institution. She reaffirmed that Clarence had been sexually inappropriate with her.

Background

In 1991, President George H.W. Bush nominated Clarence to replace Thurgood Marshall as a justice of the U.S. Supreme Court. At the time, political commentators thought that the president wanted to maintain the racial balance of the court, while adding a conservative justice who reflected the president's conservative political base. The nomination was instantly controversial. The NAACP, the National Bar Association, and the Urban League opposed the nomination out of fear that Clarence would roll back the civil rights gains for which Justice Marshall had taken major leadership. The National Organization for Woman opposed the nomination out of concerns for abortion and civil rights. Many groups and individuals were concerned about Clarence's lack of court experience. He had served for two years as a federal judge.

After a hearing within the Senate Judiciary Committee, the nomination moved to the Senate floor without a recommendation. The committee vote was split seven to seven. A few days before the final vote of the full Senate, National Public Radio and Newsday reported leaks from an FBI investigation that a co-worker had alleged that Clarence had sexually harassed her between 1981 and 1983.

Women's groups and seven women members of the U.S. House of Representatives demanded that the woman who made these allegations be asked to testify before the Senate. Anita Hill stepped forward with reluctance. For three days she testified at televised hearings. The story dominated print and electronic media in the United States and internationally for weeks.

Anita stated that Clarence had been sexually inappropriate with her after she refused to date him. He repeatedly asked her out and made sexually graphic comments and references to pornographic films. Some senators kept an open mind, and others questioned her motives. A few thought Anita might be delusional.

Clarence roared back. He denied Anita Hill's allegations and called the hearings "a high tech lynching of uppity blacks." Within days after the hearings ended, the Senate voted fifty-two to forty-eight for confirmation. Public opinion polls showed that the majority of voters supported Clarence. He did a good job of playing the race card. Counting on the Senate's fear of being perceived as racists if they did not confirm him, Clarence's use of "high tech lynching" and "uppity blacks" solidified his confirmation. Many believe the hearing was a high-tech lynching of Anita Hill.

APPLICATION OF THE THEORY

Application of the theory will show whether Clarence committed unkind deeds and then covered up.

Unkind Deeds

If Clarence had sexually harassed Anita Hill, sexual harassment is an unkind deed that he compounded because he abused his power as Anita's supervisor. He could have redeemed himself by admitting what was going on with him at the time. He may have been misguided as a younger man as to the respectful way to express romantic interest in a woman. Maybe he simply wanted to convince Anita to sleep with him. He might have used verbal sexual aggression to punish Anita for not dating him.

Perhaps growing up he had seen men behave this way toward women and get the results they wanted, or maybe he had a sense of male entitlement (a natural byproduct of a patriarchal society) that led him to believe that he could treat women any way he wanted, including abusively, with no consequences, particularly if the women are perceived to be of little value in society, as black women often are.

Motivation for Cover-Up

If Clarence was guilty of sexual harassment, his possible motivations for cover-up include face-saving and avoidance of public shame. Clarence did not mention in his 2007 interviews how controversial his nomination had been even before Anita appeared before the Senate. Picking on Anita Hill may have been a cover-up, a way to avoid being seen as the affirmative action justice of the Supreme Court.

He may have wanted to distract attention away from the possibility that other people thought of him as unqualified and that his nomination and confirmation were matters of race-based politics. He may have also feared being viewed as a "race-traitor," a "sell out," or an "uncle Tom" by African American civil rights organizations that opposed his nomination in the first place.

It is clear that racial politics had a lot to do with Clarence's nomination and confirmation. So what? As a Supreme Court justice, Clarence Thomas has had a golden opportunity to make an enormous difference in the quality of life of countless U. S. citizens, particularly those whose Constitutional rights are violated. He could have learned on the job. Instead, his decisions have led many to conclude that he has set civil rights back and will continue to do so for decades to come.

Cover-Ups

Focusing only on Anita's allegations in the 60 Minutes interview, Clarence used several different cover-ups that served to distract, distort, and shift blame and attention away from Anita's allegations. He invoked sexist stereotypes when he characterized Anita as "sensitive to slights" and "touchy." In 1991, he invoked racist stereotypes when he referred to the hearing as "a high tech lynching." These are harsh cover-ups indeed.

Buy-In

Although he won the appointment, he failed at BS in regard to Anita Hill because she had no buy-in then or now. She did not enable him to be a shit. Many other people shared Anita's views and gave her the support that helped her survive the hurt she endured.

Other people had buy-in. That Clarence became a justice and that a majority of voters supported him showed that he distracted attention away from his own scanty qualifications for highest court in the United States, not to mention his abuse of power and sexual aggression toward Anita Hill. In 1991, his behaviors were spot-on, perfect. He did what was necessary to get the job he wanted. He showed the skills of a Clever Fox. Clarence succeeded at BS in relation to the Senate and American voters who supported his confirmation. He certainly put one over on them. It is possible that the Senate was his real target and Anita was just a means to an end, collateral damage to his goal of becoming a Supreme Court judge.

Collateral Damage

In 2007, it can be argued that Clarence's behaviors fit those of a schmuck, a foolish person who refuses to take responsibility for his or her own behaviors, who shows little depth of thought, and who is insensitive to the consequences of his attack on Anita Hill. As was the case when Clarence went after the appointment to the Supreme Court, once again Anita Hill may be collateral damage in his goal to sell his book.

Clarence's knowing smile and smooth delivery during his 2007 television interview suggest that he thought he was a Clever Fox, but he may have been a True Believer. He appears to have convinced himself that his version of what happened and his views on Anita Hill are logical, true, and fitting and controversial enough to sell books, especially to the women and men who believed Anita Hill. This is Machiavellianism at its finest.

DISCUSSION

Many commentators have noted that the 1991 controversy, as hurtful as it may have been, raised awareness of sexual harassment. For example, the number of complaints to the Equal Employment Opportunity Commission doubled between 1991 and 1996. The image of a solitary young woman testifying before an all-male Senate that questioned her mental state and credibility may have been a factor in twenty-nine women being elected to the federal legislature in the years following Anita's testimony.

Whatever Clarence's motives for reviving a controversy and once more invoking sexist stereotypes to smear Anita Hill, his memoir made the *New York Times* Bestseller List. Thomas may retire from the Supreme Court a rich man. As Richard M. Nixon said, "It doesn't matter what they say about me, as long as they spell my name right." In the case of Clarence Thomas, it does not seem to matter that he has inflamed old hurts and humiliations as long as his book sells.

NINETEEN

Karl Rove Scores

K arl Rove scored seven times in one day in the game of BS. This rivals Nick's and the boyfriend's accomplishments. In three TV appearances one Sunday morning in August 2007, Rove covered up his unkind deeds like the master he is. He was the star of the hour because he had just announced his resignation as advisor to President George W. Bush. Karl used many of the cover-ups already discussed and came up with a few new ones.

Why are you picking on me? Karl asked on one of the televised news shows. He complained that the press was after him like Ahab after Moby Dick. This is similar to Don's statements that his actions were not those of a shit when they were, or like Sophie calling Bill too sensitive when she herself was insensitive. Karl is more like Ahab than the press is. Karl has an unblemished record of hounding people with whisper campaigns and innuendo, such as casting doubt on John Kerry's documented record of heroism during the Vietnamese War. Karl is so good at what he does that he made George Bush look like a hero for not showing up for his National Guard duties during the same war.

Cloaking Self in Myths and Archetypes

Karl used other tactics of cover-up. "That's not me," he said in response to his own declaration that the press had made a myth out of him when he is just a man. This is a genius-level statement because Karl cloaked himself in one of the great myths and archetypes of Western culture when he linked himself to Moby Dick. Yet, at the same time he disavowed being a myth.

"Someone else is responsible" is a phrase that Karl repeated many times, which is a version of "not me" or of deflecting blame. Asked about his awful hip-hop performance at a Radio and Television Correspondents' Association Dinner in March, Karl said, "They dragged me up there....I've got no choice...I can play along and show them that I'm a good sport." Karl said in effect that he has no will of his own, when in fact he at least gives the appearance of being the man-in-charge. He never did identify "they" and "them."

Another version of deflecting blame was Karl's statement that he had nothing to do with the outing of Valerie Plame Wilson, the undercover CIA agent, when the world believes he was at the center of it.

Karl used a version of the phrase "Everyone shares the blame" in answering a question about whether he has any responsibility in the weakening of the Republican Party. He said that every Republican ought to feel responsible. This shows mastery of the strategy of blame-shifting.

H e said the U.S. Constitution as a rule of law that tied his hands and did not allow him to comply with a Congressional subpoena in hearings on the firings of several U.S. Attorneys. Actually, the U.S. Congress has the authority to subpoena because of Constitutional checks and balances, with each of the three branches of government having oversight of the other two.

Karl used name-calling when he tagged reporters as "agents of Congress" when they asked him about his role in the firings. This makes Congress appear to be a gang of outlaws.

Karl used the "obeying orders" excuse when he responded to reporters' questions about why he subjected himself to so many question and answer shows on one day.

He said, "Somebody else made the decision for me. I'm just doing what I was instructed to do." Although such a response is not a cover-up to an unkind deed, it does show that Karl has an amazing facility to deflect responsibility for his own actions to other people, including unnamed "theys" and order-givers.

Several of these cover-ups appear "truthy." He gave his version of the truth, but he knew what the facts really were. He wanted to cast himself in the role of puppet, and unnamed persons as puppet masters. In actuality, Carl was in charge, the model for others who aspire to be puppet masters.

Karl as Master

Karl may be the master of all times of unkind deeds and cover-ups. With that said, some questions are unanswered. First, does anyone buy into his cover-ups? Huge numbers of people do. In many cases, then, Karl has succeeded in BS. For those who do not have buy-in, Karl only attained the status of bastard, hurting others and the U.S. Constitution with callous disregard.

The second question is, Does Karl think about these responses or do they arise spontaneously in his mind? Only he and maybe a few confidants know. There could be a manual somewhere that he consults. Perhaps he is writing one, an update of Machiavelli's work. Karl is a master, a genius. There is no question that he is a Clever Fox. Sit at his feet and you too will attain the Mount Olympus of BS.

PART THREE

APPLICATIONS OF THE THEORY
TO STORIES OF COMING CLEAN

On Accountability

Ella and Cara longed for reconnection with the men they loved. Neither man reconnected, but others who commit unkind deeds sometimes do. Part Three contains stories where enactors appear to realize the error of their ways, make amends, and reconnect with people they hurt. Some did so on their own. Others required pressure from many quarters. Sometimes the amends are a bit hollow, leaving the possibility that enactors are only going through the motions. They may not believe they did anything wrong and as a result take no responsibility, or they may know they did wrong but refuse to take responsibility. Whatever the case, they see no need for true amends.

TWENTY

A Daughter Steals Dad's Painting but Sees the Error of her Ways

Not all who succeed at being shits find the satisfaction they had expected. Perhaps their consciences prick them into accountability. This was the case in a story of family life that Frank Gannon wrote for a column entitled The Funny Pages in the *New York Times Magazine* about the dispute in which his two adult daughters engaged over a painting he had done thirty years before and that had been in the attic of his home since then.

After a day of wrangling that included copious use of the "f-word," Frank spied one of his daughters sneaking out of the house late at night and placing the painting in the trunk of her car. He made the decision to stay out of it and observe how things would fall out. The next day, the sisterly fight resumed with more utterances of "f-words" and confusion over the whereabouts of the painting that ended when the daughter who had stashed the painting took the high road and told her sister that if the painting were ever to be found, her sister could have it. The sibling accepted her sister's generous offer.

Confession

A few hours later, the duplicitous sister, perhaps overwhelmed with the smarminess that sometimes accompanies lying, or filled with detection apprehension, or realization that she had done something wrong and wanted to redeem herself, confessed, repented, and brought the painting back into the house. The duped sister forgave her sibling's duplicity. Gannon took the painting back. Once again, it keeps company with broken furniture and grandma's wedding dress in the attic.

This instance of BS is composed of 1) an unkind deed that consisted of sneaking the painting out of the house and hiding it, 2) a motivation to possess the painting while wanting to appear virtuous, 3) a cover-up which was the generous offer, and 4) the compliance of the sister who was hoodwinked into believing that her sibling would not be sneaky and fabricate a façade of virtue in a style that Machiavelli himself would approve.

The unsuspecting sister's trust of her duplicitous sibling is consistent with research on lying that has demonstrated how easy it is to lie to persons who trust you. Trust leads to the assumption that others would be fair. To this point, in her ingenuity and façade of altruism, the duplicitous sister has shown mastery of the high art and craft of enacting a Clever Fox style of BS in the mold of Machiavelli. Even so, her attainment of the status of shit was temporary. Without prompting from others, she gave herself up. With an admission of fault, the duplicitous sister became the prodigal sister.

Rewards of Coming Clean

The prodigal sister provided a model of the rewards of coming clean. The reward is being welcomed back into the arms of loved ones. This is repair of relationships. To do this, the prodigal sister undoubtedly had to endure her own feelings of guilt and sadness, as well as anxiety about the responses of her family. She could have had concerns about losing face. These are typical responses of liars at the prospect of having their lies unmasked and of liars who are about to expose themselves.

The prodigal sister also had to listen to words of disappointment, hurt, and even anger from her sibling and perhaps other family members before there was reconciliation. Such reproach is a natural response to duplicity as the research on lying, discussed earlier, showed. Recipients often require time to absorb the fact of a loved one's deceit.

DISCUSSION

Gannon's family saga shows a happy outcome for the sister who renounced BS and for those who love her. Their story provides a model for enactors who want to repair relationships when they commit unkind deeds and successfully cover them up.

This story shows that the value the criminal justice system places on accountability is mirrored in the value that families and friends place on accountability. By confessing, taking responsibility for their actions, and making amends individuals who commit unkind deeds and cover-ups have a good chance of being welcomed back into the fold.

TWENTY-ONE

Commentary on Accountability:
Billy Pittman's Near Perfect Apology

A pologies have several characteristics: the wrong-doer makes a full account of the unkind deeds, takes responsibility for the unkind deeds, listens to the thoughts and feelings of persons they hurt, acknowledges the hurt the unkind deeds have caused, and seeks to make amends. If the person who is wronged does not want to make amends, the now repentant wrong-doer accepts this and goes on with life.

Billy Pittman, a football player for the Longhorns at the University of Texas, provided an almost perfect example of an apology. Pittman had violated NCAA rules about personal favors when he borrowed a friend's car during the summer of 2007. He said, "I'm really sorry. It was an honest mistake, and I'll do everything I can to make up for it." What would have made the apology perfect would have been "I made a mistake. I'm really sorry. I'd do everything I can to make up for it." Then, of course, he has to mend his ways and make up for it. Saying it was an honest mistake was just a little bit of self-justification, or waffling about his accountability.

The University's Response

Borrowing the car threatened Billy's status as an amateur athlete. The athletic department and the University of Texas held him accountable. The coach suspended him for three games. The University voluntarily reported the rule violation to the college athletic association, the NCAA. Billy was on the spot. If he had not taken responsibility and apologized, he would have lost his place on the football team, his reputation would have been damaged, and he might have lost his chance for a professional football career. In some ways, he had few choices. Billy was a quick learner. He knew what he had to do.

The University was exemplary in its response to Billy's wrongdoing. The University and NCAA provided clear guidelines to Billy so he could be accountable and also salvage his reputation and keep on playing football.

Refusal of Accountability

Unlike Billy, some enactors ignore pressure and refuse to acknowledge their unkind deeds. They choose instead to fabricate a string of cover-ups. Don is an example. Even being arrested and hauled away by Dublin guards did not prompt him to acknowledge his unkind deeds and cover-ups.

When there is no pressure to reform and no apparent reward to do so, some enactors never admit they have acted like shits. Heather's boyfriend, for instance, had no other pressure than that which Heather exerted. He may even have had encouragement for his unkind deeds and cover-ups with his bar buddies. Heather gave in, but he did not. Nick only had pressure from Cara to contend with and apparently no conscience to prick him into accountability. Cara cut off contact with him and said she would be available to hear his full story. He refused.

TWENTY-TWO

Harry Dent Sees the Light

Harry Dent was a hate-mongering racist. No question. He helped construct the "Southern strategy" where politicians use code words like "states rights" and "law and order" to signal to white voters that they will not enforce laws granting voting rights and equal opportunities to African-Americans. They suggest they might even roll back the laws that are on the books. This strategy won Southern states for successful presidential candidates such as Nixon, Reagan, and Bush father and son, got Strom Thurmond elected to the U.S. Senate for decades, and has helped many other politicians, local and national, get into office.

Harry worked for Strom for several years and then worked in the Nixon White House helping to solidify the advantages won by race-based politics. He showed mastery of the cover-up when he said the Southern strategy redresses the wrongs done to white people who are left out because of affirmative action and governmental aid programs.

Harry Had Regrets

Later in life, Harry became a church deacon and helped build orphanages in Romania. He had remorse. He said, "When I look back, my biggest regret now is anything I did that stood in the way of the rights of black people, or any people." Hooray for Harry Dent. He did wrong. He committed unkind deeds and cover-ups. He realized what he had done. He acknowledged what he had done. He felt remorse. He changed his ways. He did good works. In his accountability, Harry Dent is a model for us all. His unkind deed was egregiously harmful to millions. In that, he is no model.

Harry's Status

Harry's cover-up was of the Clever Fox variety. His explanation that white people were being left out appealed to a superficial kind of fair-mindedness that in reality threatened gains that African-Americans had made toward full participation in the American dream. Both his unkind deeds and cover-ups earned him the status of bastard in the eyes of many. Those who bought into his constructions of reality enabled him to be a shit and bought into deeply-held prejudices about the worth and worthiness of African-Americans. They must have believed that they would benefit from doing so. Unkind deeds and cover-ups are rampant in political life today. The world would change if enactors mended their ways as Harry did.

TWENTY-THREE

Drug Makers Admit Guilt, but are They Sincere?

I n the face of mounting evidence, three executives of Purdue Pharma LP drug company pled guilty in May 2007 to misleading doctors and patients about the addictive qualities of a powerful painkiller called OxyContin that had earned their business about $1 billion a year for almost six years. The company pledged to pay $470 million in fines and payments to federal and state agencies and another $130 million to settle claims made by pain patients who stated they had become addicted to the drug. The executives themselves agreed to pay more than $34.5 million in fines. The charge was a misdemeanor count of mislabeling drugs.

False Representations

For more than six years, the company had advertised that OxyContin, with its time-release properties, was less addictive than fast-acting painkillers. In fact, when chewed, snorted, or injected, OxyContin produced a high as powerful as that of heroin. What's more, the company marketed the drug heavily to general practitioners who had little training or experience in managing pain and recognizing the signs of addiction. By the year 2000, addiction and crime rates associated with the narcotic soared. A spokesperson for the U.S. Justice Department's Office of Consumer Litigation said that profit was the motive for breaking the law on misleading marketing practices.

APPLICATION OF THE THEORY

The marketing of a painkiller as less addictive than competing products caused harm, including through crimes committed to obtain the drug and deaths through overdose. What's more, addiction to the drug had a bad effect on the lives of addicts, their families, and others who cared about them. Thus, the marketing and sale of a falsely labeled drug can be considered an unkind deed.

Motives for Cover-Up

The executives who covered up had advanced capacities for overlooking the consequences of the addictive qualities of the drug. They showed a moral blindness fueled by the enormous amounts of money the drug earned and by the accolades lavished on them for making so much money for shareholders and other executives. Simply put, they wanted to keep the gains earned by lies about the drug. Face-saving, too, could be a motive. They did not want to be seen as the kinds of people who would profit from a drug that causes so much damage.

Ongoing Denials

After more than eight years of wrongdoing, including at least five years of litigation, the company finally admitted its misdeeds. The fines they paid were restitution, meant perhaps to show good faith that the company executives were truly repentant. Ironically, what they paid was a fraction of the money the drug earned for the company.

Yet, a drug company spokesperson put out a press release after the verdict stating that the plea agreement did not mean there is a connection with the plea and the wide-spread addiction to the drug. He said in his written statement, "We promoted the medicine only to health-care professionals, not to consumers."

Half-Hearted Accountability

A reasonable person can question whether the drug company executives took full responsibility for their actions. From the company's point of view, their marketing had nothing to do with addiction to the drug and its consequences. Perhaps the company is blaming the doctors who prescribed the drug or the users who became addicted.

Once again, we see a situation where it is unclear whether the enactors are being accountable for their actions. They appear to be, but they also appear to be trying to save face and to absolve themselves of fault. Therefore, even though the company gave the appearance of accountability for its part in the negative consequences of its actions, its statements were half-hearted.

The Status the Executives Earned

As a result, the executives have not earned the whole hearted forgiveness of a betrayed public. Instead, they appear to have earned the status of bastards and perhaps weasels. Clearly, they have not attained the status of shits because their cover-ups were unconvincing. They were not very clever either and have not earned the status of Clever Fox, although perhaps they talked themselves into believing that the drug was not addictive. If so, they were True Believers.

TWENTY-FOUR

Oprah Winfrey
Demands Accountability

Media mogul Oprah Winfrey provided a model for how to respond when someone commits unkind deeds and then covers up. She used the direct approach of telling an enactor exactly what he had done and how what he had done had affected her and millions of others. In addition, Oprah's story shows that recipients of unkind deeds and cover-ups have a much better chance of getting enactors to admit fault when others back them up.

Oprah Lavishes Praise on a Memoir

In the fall of 2005, Oprah selected *A Million Little Pieces*, James Frey's memoir of crime, drug addiction, and recovery, for her book club, which is so popular that selected books have made millionaires of many authors. In a show called "The Man Who Kept Oprah Awake at Night," Oprah proclaimed *A Million Little Pieces* to be "like nothing you've ever read before. Everybody at Harpo[2] is reading it. When we were staying up late at night reading it, we'd come in the next morning saying, 'What page are you on?'"

The camera swung to employees who testified to the profound, life-changing revelations contained in the book. Some were in tears. Back on camera, Oprah was wiping her own eyes. She said, "I'm crying because these are all my Harpo family, and we all loved the book so much."

---

[2] This is the name of Oprah Winfrey's company. "Harpo" is "Oprah" spelled backwards.

Sitting on the white couch with Oprah, James Frey glowed with joy. Frey told Oprah. "If I was going to write a book that was true, and I was going to write a book that was honest, then I was going to have to write about myself in very, very negative ways." He said in his book, "I am an Alcoholic and I am a drug Addict and I am a Criminal." Within weeks, the book was at the top of the Net York Times best-seller list and stayed there for more than four months. Frey became a multi-millionaire.

Smoking Gun Uncovers Falsehoods

Three months later, The Smoking Gun, an Internet investigative news service, published a report called "The Man Who Conned Oprah." Through interviews with police officers and reviews of court and police reports, the report provided conclusive evidence that Frey had made up or "widely embellished" key incidents in his book. Despite the wild tales he told about his criminal career, there were no records of his alleged crimes and prison time. He was not an outlaw "wanted in three states" as he said he was. The record showed that he had spent only a few hours in jail.

The Reckoning

Immediately after the report appeared, Oprah invited James back to her show. She told James that it was hard for her to talk to him because she felt duped. She said he had betrayed millions of readers. She then asked him if the report called "The Man Who Conned Oprah" was right. James responded that most of what was in the report was "pretty accurate." Later in the interview, Oprah told James that on the earlier show, he had presented a "false person." At the end of the interview he said he had been honest with Oprah this time. "I essentially admitted to lying" were some of his final words.

His admission, however, was tainted in similar ways to the statements that Dick Cheney made about his responsibility in shooting Harry Whittington and the drug company's statement about their responsibility for the addiction of many people to OxyContin. James explained that in order for him to cope with his addiction, he thought of himself as being tougher than he actually was and as being "badder." He admitted that he might have clung to that image in writing the book rather than being "introspective."

When Oprah prompted him, he admitted he preferred to see himself that way because it would sell the book, which it certainly did. He also said that he had not conned everyone because the story he wrote was "about drug addiction and alcoholism, and nobody's disputing that I was a drug addict and an alcoholic. And it's about the battle to overcome that." Oprah was sympathetic at the end of this interview, observing how hard it must have been for James to admit that he had lied. She did not comment on the reasons he gave for lying.

Later in the show, Oprah interviewed several journalists and commentators. Most said James had not told the truth in the interview that Oprah had just conducted. One said the essential message of addiction and redemption is what counts, an argument that James had made. Someone else thought the public accountability on Oprah's show was part of James' recovery from addiction. Yet another disagreed and called James a weasel. He explained, "It's wrong and immoral to pass off a piece of fiction as a memoir."

APPLICATION OF THE THEORY

In applying the theory of BS to this scenario, James' unkind deed was to make up or embellish key incidents in the book and to pass off as factual what essentially was a fictionalized account. His motives for embellishing key events, he said, were to sell books and to help him cope with his addiction

When Oprah confronted him, he admitted he had lied. Before then, others had questioned him, and he repeatedly said he had told the truth. His motive for this cover-up, perhaps, was to save face and to keep selling books. Even in the interview with Oprah, he minimized the seriousness of the lies and justified them. James was a bit short of full accountability.

Oprah Refused Buy-In

Oprah, however, had no buy-in to James' justifications. She believed the Smoking Gun Report. She waffled when she said that it must have been hard for him to admit that he had lied. She also did not attempt to force him to admit that any excuse or minimization spoiled his statement of accountability. In some respects, it does not matter whether enactors of unkind deeds and cover-ups admit the full extent of their wrongdoing. What does matter is that recipients figure out what's going on and refuse buy-in.

In the end, James failed at BS. Those who thought James was not justified in making things up were not duped. Those who thought it was okay to make things up obviously did not care that he had. The journalist who called James a weasel used the same term I would to describe James' actions. He partially redeemed himself when he admitted before millions that the book was largely made up.

DISCUSSION

This story, like several others, shows how slippery accountability can be. True accountability does not involve excuses or rationalizations. Those who are accountable say, "I was wrong. I'm sorry. I want to make up for what I did. I hope you can forgive me." These are simple words, but difficult for many people. Some mistake accountability for weakness or believe they will be treated unfairly if they admit fault. Others know that they will have to face consequences and do not want to do this. Some want to save face and manage impressions. Still others want to keep their gains, a portion of whom have no shame about what they did to get what they have. Finally, there are those who truly believe they did nothing wrong.

Whatever motivates enactors, the high road is the willingness toentertain the notion that you could do something wrong and even harmful, to listen to others who may be telling you something important about your actions, to be accountable, to accept consequences, to make things right, and to reconnect whenever possible.

TWENTY-FIVE

Commentary on the Differences Between True and Fake Accountability

H ow to tell true accountability from fake requires the wit of a Clever Fox. Duplicitous enactors give the appearance of accountability, and they often declare their sincere sorrow. Such actions instill hope that they are accountable and will change their ways.

Some enactors learn to fake accountability while young. An example is an older sibling who torments younger siblings when the parents are not present. The younger children complain to parents who insist that the older child apologize. The apology is duly offered, but as soon as the parents are absent, the older child once again mocks, teases, and harasses the younger children. The apology meant nothing.

Nick displayed fake accountability on at least two occasions. The first was when he declared himself a bastard who had hurt Cara and the second was when he said he would be glad to answer questions about Moira. He neither stopped being a bastard nor did he answer any questions. He did not follow through on his words. Therefore, a principle that separates fake accountability from true is whether enactors desist from unkind deeds and cover-ups in the future.

Completeness of Descriptions

A second principle useful in the test of whether accountability is fake or sincere is the completeness of enactors' descriptions of their unkind deeds and cover-ups. For example, Dick Cheney gave the appearance of contrition in his shooting of Harry Whittington, but he did not state that he and not Harry broke the rules of hunting. He did nothing to erase the initial statements of his spokespeople that Harry had broken the rules of hunting and he, Dick, had done nothing wrong. Setting the record straight would have been a more complete account of the incident and its aftermaths. Harry cooperated by commiserating with Dick's ordeal and overlooking his own.

First-Person Statements

A third principle that separate true accountability from fake is whether enactors state that they are responsible and not some vague group of unnamed individuals. Vagueness gives the appearance of honesty, but is in fact a deflection of responsibility. The phrase "mistakes were made" accomplishes this. U.S. Attorney General Alberto Gonzales uttered this phrase when he attempted to convince the press, the nation, and maybe even other parts of the world that he took responsibility for the firing of eight U.S. attorneys in the fall of 2006.

Had he said, "I made mistakes," then he might have convinced others that he was being accountable. He then explained that he has more than one hundred thousand people under his command and that he delegates many tasks, including the task of firing the attorneys. Someone among the one hundred thousand apparently made a mistake, but not Mr. Gonzales.

"Mistakes were made" is like a mantra among persons who want to save face by faking their way out of having their cover-ups exposed. Paul Wolfowitz insisted that the phrase "mistakes were made all around" be inserted into the documents that described why he left as president of the World Bank in May 2007. His mistake was to approve a huge raise for his life partner who worked for the bank. What appeared in the document was "a number of mistakes were made by a number of individuals." Who made the mistakes, when, and for what purpose are unstated.

Paul further whitewashed his mistakes by making sure that the World Bank statement listed his accomplishments as president. By so doing and by being vague about who was at fault, Paul provided a model of what enactors of unkind deeds and cover-ups can do to save face when they are found out. As John Broder noted in a *New York Times* article, the phrase "mistakes were made" is a "familiar fallback" among politicians. Broder listed several politicians who used that phrase to weasel out of taking personal responsibility for their behaviors. They included Richard M. Nixon, Ronald Reagan, and Bill Clinton.

Acceptance of Recrimination

Accountable persons listen to and hear what the persons they hurt have to say. This is the fourth principle of accountability. As research on lying shows, backed up by common sense, when liars are found out, recipients are hurt, sad, and full of recrimination. The only way for enactors of unkind deeds and cover-ups to know how their behaviors affected others would be to listen carefully and really hear what others say. It is not easy to face up to hurt and anger that one has caused. The reward is a clear conscience, even if recipients are not ready to carry on with a relationship. In many cases, listening and hearing leads to relationship repair.

DISCUSSION

Four principles guide enactors who want to be accountable for their unkind deeds and cover-ups: sincerity, completeness, clarity, and acceptances of recrimination. Doing so is not easy. For many enactors, becoming accountable requires them to examine and transform their beliefs about who they are. Some may believe admitting fault is a sign of weakness. They refuse to be accountable out of fear of appearing weak. In actuality, accountable persons recognize that it takes courage to admit wrongdoing. They know they are risking a great deal when they do so. Those who do not see accountability as an act of courage miss out on the relief and joy of coming clean. They are stuck with the smudges and smarminess that go along with unkind deeds and cover-ups.

TWENTY-SIX

What Not to Do: Jimmy Carter Waffles

F ormer President Jimmy Carter provided a model of what not to do when enactors blow back. Blowback is kind of "super" cover-up that arises when enactors realize their unkind deeds are about to be exposed. Blowback is a reaction to detection apprehension meant to intimidate resisters into backing down.

In the summer of 2007, Carter was unprepared for the responses directed at him after he famously criticized the administration of George W. Bush as the "worst in history" in terms of its "adverse impact around the world." A Bush White House spokesperson had an immediate blowback: Tony Fratto said Carter's words are "sad and reckless evidence" that Carter is "increasingly irrelevant." Fox News joined in the blowback. They stated that Carter's "administration was plagued by sky-high inflation and a 444-day American hostage crisis in Iran." They failed to note Carter's accomplishments.

Rollback

The next day in a nationally televised interview, Carter tried to take back some of what he had said. He characterized his remarks as "maybe careless or misinterpreted." He wanted to be sure that other people understood that he was only comparing Bush's policies to those of Nixon. Several commentators said that in this electronic age there was no way he could take back his earlier words.

The day after Carter's attempt to roll back his words, President Bush delivered a soft blowback when he said his (Bush's) "actions are based on what's best for this country." Tony Fratto said of Carter's rollback on his criticism of Bush, this "just highlights the importance of being careful in choosing your words." Tony chose his own words so carefully that Machiavelli would be proud.

ANALYSIS

In actuality, Carter had a point. At the time of Carter's criticism, the foreign policy of the United States was held in grave disfavor throughout the world, especially for the invasion of Iraq. Had Bush and members of his administration chosen to be accountable, they would have said that they take the words of an esteemed elder statesman seriously. They would have promised to look into the truth of what Carter said and report back to a national and international audience.

Instead, a spokesperson attacked Carter and Bush took the "high road" of virtue that Machiavelli recommended. Fox News responded with innuendo and the omission of information, tactics that betray journalistic principles of balanced and fair reporting. This is truthiness in full flower. Such responses were hardball that must have been direct hits at the hot buttons of the elder statesman. They were a cover-up that diverted attention from Carter's criticism.

Carter Had Backup, but Too Late

Carter had the backup of many after he voiced his criticism. For example, Senator Hillary Rodham Clinton refused to condemn Carter's views and said the Iraq policy has failed, President Bush is stubborn, the Iraqi government is unwilling to make "tough decisions" and as a result "our young women and men are in harm's way."

In a story that appeared in the *Nation*, the commentator John Nichols praised Carter for his astute interpretation of the Bush policies and noted that the presidential spin machine roared into overdrive when the enormously popular Jimmy Carter pointed out the obvious. Calling the present administration "very touchy," Nichols said that Jimmy Carter's "approval ratings dwarf those of George Bush these days."

Waffling vs. Staying the Course

Carter waffled and Oprah Winfrey stayed the course. Perhaps the differences between the two, both of whom publicly criticized other people for their actions, are the degree of support they had before they spoke up. Oprah had a multitude behind her. Jimmy Carter acted alone. By the time support arose, he had already tried to take back his words. Had Carter known how strong his support was, he might have stood firm when the president's spokespeople hit back. Oprah had little if any blowback. James' contrition and embarrassment could have been a soft kind of blowback that might have influenced Oprah to sympathize with James over how difficult the interview must have been. Yet, she did not roll back her stand that he had lied.

Resisters in Harm's Way

Resistance to cover-ups can put resisters in harm's way. Those who blow back can be Clever Foxes who intentionally strike resisters' vulnerabilities and then enjoy what happens next. Even Reactors and True Believers may hammer at vulnerabilities, whether by accident or intuition. Preparation for blowback may be a wise course of action when recipients want to call someone to account for unkind deeds and cover-ups.

PART FOUR

CONCLUSIONS,
OR WHERE DO WE GO FROM HERE?

With Jimmy Carter's story, the testing of the preliminary theory is complete. I now present the reformulation of the theory in light of the analysis, report on new learnings that result from the analysis, and discuss the implications of this research.

TWENTY-SEVEN

The Final Version of the Theory

T he present study developed and tested a theory of BS. Its four components held up well, especially the idea that enactors cannot achieve the status of shit without the cooperation of recipients. Therefore, I have no evidence that necessitates changing the core of the theory.

The final version is as follows. BS is composed of four parts:

1. an unkind deed
2. a desire to evade responsibility for the unkind deed
3. a cover-up, and
4. recipient buy-in.

While the core of the theory remains the same, the analysis revealed unanticipated aspects of BS that add notable dimensions. These aspects include the discovery of new types of cover-up, the significance of the lesser statuses, the resistance that some enactors mount, and the joys of BS. In addition, testing of the theory shows that the same enactor can be a Reactor at some points, a True Believer at others, and a Clever Fox at still other times.

TWENTY-EIGHT

New Types of Cover-Up

T his study began with the identification of such cover-ups as humor, duplicity, withholding information, minimization, prevarication, facial expressions, shaming, blaming, and name-calling. While conducting the analysis, I identified additional cover-ups including indignation, silence, mockery, gaslighting, cut-offs, threats to abandon, "I can't recall," "Mistakes were made," and "What do you expect?" Table 1 in the Appendix lists these cover-ups and those who used them.

Noteworthy Cover-Ups

Heather's boyfriend was a master gaslighter. His slights of hand, mockery, and minimizations led to questions she could not withstand. How important is a coffee grinder? What really matters? These questions minimized his unkind deeds, and by asking them, the boyfriend activated Heather's hot buttons. She was undone. She could not match wits with this Clever Fox.

Acting hurt and innocent and then walking out in indignation are other tactics the preliminary theory did not anticipate. The boyfriend did this after watching Heather "tear the apartment apart" for two days looking for the grinder. Don used this tactic as well when he chastised Ella for asking him if he still slept with his wife. He delivered the knockout blow when he stomped out. Ella ran after him, begging forgiveness. False hurt, indignation, attacking others, threats of abandonment, cover-ups indeed. They work. The crowning achievement of being is shit is to convince other people that they are at fault.

Karl Rove and Alberto Gonzales used variations of these tactics, which helped them to succeed at getting what they wanted for a long time, but in the end, they both resigned from office after pressure from many quarters to do so.

Cover-Ups Change Shape

Cover-ups, like unkind deeds continually change shape. Just when you think you have heard them all, creative enactors come up with new ones. For example, days before this book was going to press, I discovered a variation called "I want it both ways." Allen Raymond, a consultant for the Republican Party, served three months in a federal prison for jamming the phone lines of the Democratic get-out-the vote effort in the 2002 New Hampshire elections. On contract with the New Hampshire Republican party, Allen claimed that an executive of the Republican National Committee (RNC) asked him to jam the phone lines and someone from the New Hampshire Republican party gave him the phone numbers.

The executive was convicted in a lower court and acquitted on appeal. The RNC paid for his defense, but not for Allen's. Allen said the Committee defended the other man because they "wanted him to keep his yap shut" about who was responsible for the dirty trick.

Allen pled guilty. He told the judge, "Your Honor, I did a bad thing. While what I did was outside my character, I take full responsibility for my actions." At the same hearing, Allen's lawyer tried to absolve Allen. He said, "This was not Allen Raymond's idea." It was the RNC executive's idea. The judge asked, "What about a personal moral compass?"

B itter about the RNC's failure to defend him, Allen complained that the Committee "not only threw me under the bus but then blamed me for getting run over." With this statement and the statement of his attorney, Allen undermined his own declaration of full responsibility. These words also describe the actions of a shit, although he avoided the use of that word, at least in public. Allen did not keep his "yap" shut. In

2008, he published a book called *How to Rig an Election*. Like Bill in regard to Sophie, Allen may be motivated by revenge. On the other hand, if he contributes to electoral reform, he is doing a great service.

TWENTY-NINE

The Resistance
that Some Recipients Mount

A nother unanticipated finding was the resistance that some recipients mount. In some instances, resistance was successful for a time but eventually recipients caved in. Others enabled cover-ups until they finally realized that enactors were trying to hoodwink them, sometimes in soft, humorous ways and sometimes harshly. A few recipients had no buy-in and resisted throughout the course of the enactments of unkind deeds and cover-ups.

Resistance and Then Giving In

Heather showed admirable resistance to her boyfriend's constructions of reality, but she eventually saw things as her boyfriend intended. Being cozy in bed with him may have meant more than insisting that he stop playing her. She never let on whether the boyfriend was accountable in the coffee grinder caper.

Giving In and Then Resistance

Ella and Cara successfully enabled their lovers' unkind deeds and cover-ups many times, but by the end, they realized that the men they had loved were not who they thought they were. They walked away.

Balanced Responses

Another pattern of resistance is exemplified in Hamish MacBeth's rational and balanced responses to Jamie's accusations and expostulations. Instead of undoing Hamish, Jamie found himself unmasked and undone. The cool elegance of Hamish's dealings with Jamie suggested the finesse of a Clever Fox. This case led to the speculation that successful resisters must possess skills that exceed those of enactors. Hamish had the skills of a Clever Fox put to pro-social ends. These skills exceeded Jamie's self-serving True Believer actions.

Oprah Winfrey provided yet another case of exemplary behavior. James Frey duped her. She felt betrayed. She told him so clearly and in detail on national television. She was widely praised for admitting that she had made a mistake in promoting James' book and wide-spread praise in confronting him about his lies.

<h2>LESSONS FOR RESISTERS</h2>

The stories examined in this research have lessons for people who want to unmask unkind deeds and cover-ups.

Have Credible Evidence

First, make sure you have evidence. Oprah had evidence in the form of the Smoking Gun report. Few of us in our personal or professional lives will have this much evidence of the wrongdoings of others. Sometimes we are unsure whether our evidence is credible. In such cases, it is important to talk to impartial people to see what they think. The evidence we have could be distorted. It could be incomplete. Evidence must withstand the scrutiny of unbiased persons. The Smoking Gun report was credible because of the thoroughness of the investigation the news group mounted.

Have Backup

Second, have backup. It is difficult to stand up to cover-up alone, especially if enactors' cover-ups are harsh and accusatory but also if the cover-ups play on our sympathy, desires to please others, or our longing for peace. Oprah had a national and even international audience who agreed that she had credible evidence and that she was right to confront the man who had duped her. With that many people as backup, it was unlikely she would fail. In her strategies, Oprah exemplified a Clever Fox style of resistance that, in combination with evidence, wore James Frey down. Few of us will have such extensive backup when we have credible evidence that unmasks unkind deeds and cover-ups. However, it is wise to have at least a few people to back us up.

Those who have succeeded at being shits, whether Reactors, True Believers, or Clever Foxes, can be powerful in their efforts to discredit their critics. Jimmy Carter found that Fox News and White House aides declared him to be at fault. Indirectly, President Bush did, too. Few people can stand up to blowback as lone rangers.

In some cases, enactors who blow back have widespread support in social customs and traditions. Heather found that the research she consulted about relationship conflict put the blame on her. Jamie the failed scriptwriter and Clarence Thomas invoked woman-hating stereotypes of "bitch" and "sensitive to slights." Brad called Marvin a sissy, and Sophie told Bill he was too sensitive. These words struck at vulnerabilities related to beliefs about proper male conduct. Given the power of customs and beliefs, backup can mean the difference between resistance and capitulation.

Prepare

Third, prepare for many possible responses. Resisters are in strong positions if they are ready for anything. Sometimes enactors take immediate responsibility, apologize, and seek to reconnect. Sometimes enactors break off the relationship. That is what Nick did when Cara pressed him for details on what Moira meant to him. Some enactors go on the offense and attack in emotionally abusive ways, as Jamie did to Angus and Fiona and the White House spokespersons and some of the media did to Jimmy Carter. A few enactors degenerate into pitiful creatures, such as Don when the Dublin guards hauled him off. In some cases, blowback could take the form of physical violence. Once again, here is a reason for individuals to have the support of others when they want to unmask cover-ups of unkind deeds.

Preparation for any of these outcomes will enable recipients to stay the course and not cave as Heather eventually did to her boyfriend's constructions of reality. Jimmy Carter, too, appeared to give in at least to some degree to the blowback he received.

Accept Consequences

Fourth, accept negative consequences. Resistance involves risk. Cara, for example, lost Nick, and Ella lost Don. Both thought themselves better off, but the loss was painful. On the other hand, pride in staying the course can offset negative consequences, as was the case for Cara and Ella, and I hope for Anita Hill. Whether responses are soft or harsh, enactors can be formidable in their blowback. Resistance that stays the course is something to celebrate. Sometimes other people celebrate as well. Oprah received wide recognition for her resistance to James Frey's misrepresentations.

WISDOM IS KNOWING WHAT TO OVERLOOK

In some instances, recipients may refuse buy-in, but they chose to overlook enactors' unkind deeds and cover-ups. When this happens, my hope is that they do so with the wit and mindfulness of a Clever Fox. By this I mean that they realize that they have overlooked something but it is worth it. In some cases, the behaviors are minor and of little importance. The benefits of keeping the relationship outweigh small irritants. This may have been the case for Heather. The question of "How important is it?" is worth asking. In other instances, enactors must change their behaviors to restore trust. Finally, there are those who refuse accountability, and their actions are serious enough for recipients to end relationships.

THIRTY

Significance of the Lesser Statuses

T he testing of the preliminary theory provided evidence that terms considered and then discarded in favor of *shit* actually have a place in the theory. The terms *prick, schmuck,* and *weasel* fit the statuses of those who fail at being shits and, as a result, earned their way into the theory. The status enactors attain depends upon the nature of their cover-ups and upon the nature of their unkind deeds. In addition, partway into the analysis, I realized that the actions of the coal mine owners and their governmental confederates fit the word *bastard,* when it is used to mean callousness and entitlement. The mean-spiritedness of their cover-ups and the nature of their unkind deeds entitled them to this status.

Beside those involved in the coal mining cover-ups, many other enactors succeeded at being bastards, the lawyer Laura and her confederates, Jamie the scriptwriter, Don who was Ella's lover, and Nick who was Cara's lover. Each was callous. They believed themselves to be entitled to act as they did and to reap the benefits of their actions. They did whatever it took to cover-up. With such strong evidence, I included this term in the theory.

Alternate Statuses Depends Upon Enactors

The actions of recipients bring about failures at being shits, but the actions of enactors determine which alternative statuses they achieve. Many stories show this, such as Don's and Ella's. When Ella refused to buy into Don's cover-ups, Don's behaviors at first entitled him to the status of bastard, with his final achievement that of the lowly weasel, a satisfying ending for readers who saw through Don the whole time and who rooted for Ella to do the same.

Cara, stunned by Nick's refusal to answer any more questions, realized Nick was not who she thought he was. As she worked toward a new understanding of Nick's character, the harshness of his actions convinced her that she had come to the end of the road with him. Without Cara's buy-in, Nick's status became that of bastard—callous, unrepentant, and unaccountable. The flowery birthday card was an indicator that he also could be clueless about the effects of his actions. Nick in this instance was a True Believer of the bastard type.

A Hierarchy of Enactors

Earlier, I had speculated that the statuses of shit, bastard, prick, schmuck, and weasel form a hierarchy, where BS is the highest status that enactors can achieve and weasel the lowest. When I first proposed this status hierarchy, I was in the midst of testing the preliminary theory, which did not account for what to call persons who fail at being shits.

I now have evidence that supports this speculation. I found many instances where enactors succeeded when recipients had buy-in, and other instances where recipients resisted buy-in and enactors achieved other statuses. The status of bastard might be the most common, followed by prick, schmuck, and weasel. I also found that the statuses enactors achieved depended upon their own actions.

Although I identified few schmucks, I believe this is a matter of perspective. James Frey, in many ways, fits the definition of schmuck, as I believe many other enactors do as well, including Nick and Jamie. Karl Rove could well fit the category of schmuck, especially when he claimed that other people made him do it. Figure 1 shows the arrangement of these statuses in a hierarchy with the highest achievement at the top and the lowest at the bottom. BS is at the pinnacle, symbolizing what an accomplishment that status is. Following BS in order are bastard, prick, and schmuck. Weasel is at the bottom of the hierarchy, signifying the lowly status the term designates.

Further research may refine this status hierarchy or even refute it. All research findings, no matter how derived, are subject to modification when scientists identify new evidence. That is how science proceeds—from conjecture or theory, to theory testing, to modification or refutation of theory, and reformulation, as previously discussed.

Variety in the Lesser Statuses

Earlier, I had also hypothesized that the lesser statuses could come in the same varieties as those of shit. I now have evidence that supports this speculation. For example, at the end of *Quentins*, Don was a weasel of the Reactor type. Jamie was a schmuck and weasel who also may have been a True Believer as well as Reactor. Sophie and Bill achieved the status of bastard of the Reactor type. Karl Rove was a Clever Fox to the end, but he also may be a weasel, schmuck, and prick. Karl once again hit the jackpot.

Finally, the application of the preliminary theory to stories shows that enactors can shift between being Reactors, True Believers, and Clever Foxes. They can also succeed at being shits at some points, but then also find that when recipients refuse buy-in, their own actions relegate them to the ranks of bastard, prick, schmuck, and weasel. These ranks can change depending upon their own actions. Recipients have the power to dethrone them from being shits, but their own actions determine the statuses they achieve. No one can succeed at BS without the consent of recipients.

THIRTY-ONE

The Joys of BS

An unanticipated finding was that some people enact being shits for the joy of it. The preliminary theory foreshadowed a degree of delight in regard to Clever Foxes, who enjoy putting one over on other people. Impression management, face-saving, and evasion of consequences, however, were the main motivations I identified in the preliminary theory. Unexpectedly, the joys of BS emerged as a key motivation in many of the stories. In fact, five patterns of joy earned their way into the revised theory.

Duping Delight

The first pattern is enjoyment that is similar to Ekman's notion of duping delight. In this pattern, enactors are obvious about their delight. Representing this pattern are Heather's boyfriend and Brad, who made fun of Marvin and his mother Margaret. Both appeared to have enjoyed themselves enormously, Heather's boyfriend in quite subtle ways by facial expressions, body language and soft, mocking tones. Brad, being younger, was more overt in his delight. He giggled as he mocked others, egged on undoubtedly by his appreciative audience.

Heather's boyfriend may have played to an imaginary audience who applauded his cleverness in fooling Heather so completely. It is possible that he had a real audience of cronies at a bar somewhere in New York City. He plucked Heather's strings and pushed her buttons. He played her, and she moved in rhythm to his whims.

Covert Joy

The second pattern involves covert joy in enacting and getting away with unkind deeds and cover-ups, covert because enactors do not show their joy in any way. Examples of this second pattern are 1) Laura the attorney's triumph over Sabrina who had brought an unlawful discharge lawsuit against her former employers, 2) the strip coal mine owners who absolved themselves of responsibility for property damage and gross disrespect for residents and their land, and 3) Sophie who fooled Bill into thinking that he was too sensitive when, from some points of view, she was inconsiderate and a bit of a bastard and perhaps a weasel for not taking responsibility for the mouth debris she had spit onto the bathroom sink. Karl Rove, too, and the drug company executives may be of this variety.

Clarence Thomas could have taken enormous satisfaction in his appointment as justice of the U. S. Supreme Court after characterizing the Senate hearings as "a high tech lynching of uppity blacks." This ploy distracted attention away from his lack of qualifications and the doubts that Anita Hill's testimony raised about his character. These words also activated the hot buttons of some senators that led them to fear that other people would perceive them as racists.

Laura, the strip mine owners, the governmental officials, Sophie, and Clarence, did not show explicit joy in their accomplishments, but it makes sense that they gained satisfaction from getting what they wanted. Furthermore, Laura, her law firm, and the coal mine owners also benefited materially, earning a great deal of money as a result of their unkind deeds and cover-ups. Possessing material wealth is a source of joy and satisfaction for many, if for no other reason than they can flaunt their wealth to real and imaginary audiences.

Fun and Then a Crash

The third pattern is when enactors appear to have fun for a time, perhaps even experience duping delight, only to crash and burn eventually. For example, Jamie appeared to have enjoyed his fame and acclaim, but he ended up murdered in the Scottish Highlands. The men who wanted two women may have had a wonderful time, first, enjoying the company of two women and, next, getting away with something they knew would be met with disapproval if their deeds came to light. In Don's case, he flew high for a while, but fell apart in his last scenes with Ella and exhibited the actions of a weasel. Nick may have enjoyed his little harem for many years. How long, he never said. Karl Rove, too, may have had years of joy at getting away with BS. During the final months of being Bush's advisor, however, so many journalists and politicians demanded accountability that it is unlikely that Karl enjoyed himself as much as he once had.

Enjoyment and then Repentance

The fourth pattern involves enactors who enjoyed themselves temporarily, but repent. They not only tell on themselves, but they also take responsibility for their deeds, accept consequences, and then seek reconnection with those whom they had duped. Harry Dent is an example of someone who committed serious unkind deeds that were not illegal, who gained enormously not only for himself but for the politicians for whom he worked, and who in later life saw the error of his ways. He admitted that he had done wrong, repented, and attempted to live an exemplary life afterward.

Another enactor who repented was the duplicitous sister who hid her father's painting in her car and faked the moral high ground by telling her sister that if the painting ever turned up her sister could have it, an unkind, sneaky cover-up if there ever was one. She may have experienced temporary delight and joy over the theft and duplicity as well as the anticipation of having the prized painting in her possession. The duplicitous sister unmasked herself, possibly in response to the pricking of her conscience, or the smudge and smarmy feeling that DePaulo and colleagues identified in their research on lying. Her loving family received her like the prodigal she was.

The duplicitous sister's behaviors led to the best outcome possible when one has succeeded at BS. How difficult the path of coming clean can be, however. To follow it, enactors must relinquish the much-sought prize whatever it may have been, admit to the people they have hurt that they have committed unkind deeds, and endure the recrimination of recipients before reconciliation is possible. In some cases, recipients may not want reconciliation, although some may grant it eventually.

A variation on renouncing the joys of BS in favor of repentance is found in James Frey's story. In response to great pressure, James came clean in a most public way, which must have been hard, but in the long run, he appears to have lost nothing and may have gained a great deal. Not only did James have a fine time getting wealthy and famous based on a book that was a fictionalized account and not a memoir, but after his public repentance, his book continued to sell, he is still famous and wealthy, and he continues to do work that interests him. Within months after his comeuppance from Oprah, he received a contract worth millions for his next book. Finally, his public admission of lying could have been a boost in James' recovery from addiction, since recovery requires accountability.

The stories about James, Harry Dent, and the duplicitous sister show good things happen when enactors take responsibility for their behaviors. For the sister, reconnection with her family may have been worth giving up any benefits gained by success at BS. The same could be said of James and Harry.

Absence of Joy or Delight

The fifth pattern is when enactors experience an absence of joy in getting away with something. The cover-up following Dick Cheney's shooting of Harry Whittington is an example. Dick's spokespeople may not have enjoyed themselves as they covered up why Dick had not contacted the news media immediately after the shooting. Of course, they themselves had not shot Harry, so they actually did not enact being shits in a full sense. Willing or not, they were part of the cover-up and facilitated someone else's success. Dick himself did not appear to experience joy at getting away with his cover-ups. His statement that no one was at fault but himself was joyless. He did not even seem to enjoy leaving uncorrected the earlier impression that Harry had broken the rules of hunting and he, Dick, was blameless. Like Dick, Alberto Gonzales did not appear to have enjoyed himself or to have experienced duping delight, even when he succeeded with his unkind deeds and cover-ups.

SUMMARY

Many enactors enjoy themselves as they get away with their unkind deeds. I have identified five patterns with some variations within patterns. There may be even more types of joy related to BS. As mentioned, BS appears to be protean. There is little reason to doubt that the benefits of BS are protean as well. Future research will contribute further knowledge about the joys of BS.

THIRTY-TWO

Final Thoughts

When recipients of unkind deeds refuse buy-in to cover-ups, enactors fail at being shits, but succeed as bastards, pricks, schmuck, and weasels. What lesser statuses enactors attain depends upon their own words and actions. Recipients are in powerful positions because no one can succeed at BS without their consent.

Enactors are on their way to success when recipients wonder what THEY did wrong. In reality, recipients may have done nothing wrong. If they feel guilty, they can ask trusted others, "Is it me?" If they find they are in the wrong, they can be accountable. If their guilt and shame are misplaced, they will see the unkind deeds and cover-ups for what they are.

It can be hard for recipients to believe that people they love and trust commit unkind deeds and then cover-up. Many recipients prefer to blame themselves rather than think ill of someone else. What's more, it is not unusual for other people to blame recipients and let enactors off the hook.

At times, standing up to unkind deeds and cover-ups sets off hot buttons that raise fears of blowback. Recipients remain silent to avoid these consequences. Sometimes recipients have solid grounds for their fears because some blowback is seriously harmful. At other times, their fears are connected to earlier painful and confusing experiences and have nothing to do with present circumstances. These responses may lead recipients to appease rather than hold enactors

Enactors

Through my research on the meanings of violence to perpetrators, I have listened to thousands of stories that show how selfish and self-centered some people can be. Many do not think about the effects of their behaviors on others. Recipients are collateral damage. Some minimize the gravity of what they have done. Some do not care. Some even enjoy hurting others. They laugh. They get a rush. Some enactors cherish resistance because it gives them reason to roar back. Blowback is fun for them. Finally, some enactors are genuinely confused human beings who, with some help, can learn to be accountable.

Detection

Recipients can use the present theory to test whether or not someone else is BS. Did the other person commit an unkind deed? Do they have reason to hide what they did? What did they do to cover-up? How did their actions affect recipients? These questions can help detect BS. Individuals can use the theory of BS on their own actions. Many believe they have a lot to lose if they become accountable, but when they stop dumping on others, they will find that life lightens up. Repentance and reconnection are their own rewards.

Revenge

Recipients who become enactors are part of a chain of unkind deeds and cover-ups where recipients and enactors switch roles. As good as revenge may feel, it is a temporary solution and becomes part of the problem. Accountability stops the cycle of BS.

More to be Learned

There is more to be learned. BS appears in many forms and truly is a shape-shifter. To outwit them, recipients must have the skills of Clever Foxes and be willing to face facts. Some people, including people they know and love, may enact unkind deeds and cover-ups and let recipients feel as if they have done something wrong. The present research is an important move toward understanding a pervasive human condition. Further research will test the results of this investigation and undoubtedly will come up with new evidence that will lead to revisions of the theory.

APPENDICES

Table 1: A List of Cover-Ups and their Enactors

Further Details on Method

Endnotes

About the Author

Table 1: A List of Enactors and their Cover-Ups

Actions

Nick	hanging up the phone
Heather's boyfriend	walking away
Don	walking away

Blaming

Nick	"What do you expect?"
Sophie	"You're too sensitive."
Bill	"You asked for it."
Thérèse	"You won. You have what you wanted."
Heather's boyfriend	"You have no idea what really matters
Mine owners	property previously damaged.
Jamie	"Get the police."
Don	"Someone must have hurt you."
Don	"Shame on you for your lack of faith in me"
Karl Rove	"just following orders"
Karl Rove	"Every Republican ought to feel responsible"
Karl Rove	"Someone else made me do it"

Blowback

Tony Fratto	irrelevance of Carter's opinion
Fox News	Carter's sorry record as president
George W. Bush	protecting the country for the American people

Criticizing other people for what enactors do

Karl Rove	The press is after me
Nick	cyberstalking
Jamie	Angus as bastard

Table 1: A List of Enactors and their Cover-Ups (*Continued*)

Facial Expressions

Heather's boyfriend	"stare of infinite Buddhist compassion"
Nick	impish look

Fake Accountability

Nick	"I'm a bastard. I hurt you."

Gaslighting

Heather's boyfriend	No wonder you can't find anything -
Nick	"I'm not answering any more questions."
Nick	birthday card meant nothing

Humor

Nick	two women as not much of a harem
Click or Clack	car ran funny when it did not
George W. Bush	rolled eyes and laughed

"I cannot recall."

Richard M. Nixon
Nick
Attorney General Gonzales

Indignation

Nick	"Who told you?"
Jamie	"How dare you!"
Clarence Thomas	"high tech lynching of uppity blacks"
Karl Rove	The press is after me

Minimization

Heather's boyfriend	"You have no idea what really matters"

Nick   "Life is a mystery"
Katherine Armstrong   "little-bitty pellets"
Katherine Armstrong   Harry sitting up in bed, yakking
Harry Whittington   empathy for Dick Cheney

"Mistakes were made."
Attorney General Gonzales
Paul Wolfowitz

Mockery
Heather's boyfriend   Who moved my cheese?"
Heather's boyfriend   body language, tone of
voice
Brad   "Stick your head in, you
                                            clam."

Name-Calling
Nick   "cyber stalker"
Sophie   "You're too sensitive"
Brad   "fem" and "clam"
Jamie   "useless wee faggot",
                                        "bastard," and "bitch"

Heather's boyfriend   "nutty"
Clarence Thomas   "touchy" & "sensitive to
slights"
Karl Rove   "agents of Congress"

Prevarication
Alicia   "I'm going to a meeting."
Nick   "She is not permanent."
Nick   "I'm with you now. Where
is
                                            she?"
Heather's boyfriend   had not seen the cover
grinder

Truthiness
Dick Cheney   No one else is responsible.
Fox News   Carter's sorry record as
president

146

Swiftboating

Thérèse
wanted

You've got what you

Threats of abandonment

Nick
Don
to

cut off communication
"We don't have anything

talk about, do we?"

Withholding Information

The son
Laura
Jamie
Dick Cheney and
Dick's spokespeople

no mention of bad fuel in tank
why Sabrina was late
authorship of the script
not correcting earlier statements that Harry had not followed the rules of
hunting and Dick had

Heather's boyfriend
Heather's boyfriend
Nick
Duplicitous sister

whereabouts of coffee grinder
the replacement of the grinder
place of Moira in his life
the location of the painting

I Want it Both Ways

Allen Raymond

"They threw me under the bus."
"I take full responsibility."

Further Details on Method

In this section are further details on deductive qualitative analysis (DQA), the method I used to develop and test a theory of BS. In DQA, researchers begin with a preliminary theory that can be composed of loosely formulated hunches based on personal or professional experience, formal hypotheses, or a set of ideas that form a model of how things work (Gilgun, 2005c).

In the present study, the preliminary theory was based on research I had conducted previously, my professional experience as a social worker, my personal observations over many years, a review of the uses and meanings of the term *shit*, and a review of research on related phenomena. Insights from cognitive neuroscience added to the preliminary theory.

Researchers test the preliminary theory through surveys, experiments, or case studies. In the present research, I tested the theory on cases, which were stories of everyday life that I took from many different sources. When the theory does not fit findings, the theory is changed.

DQA is an updating of analytic induction, a form of qualitative inquiry that researchers at the University of Chicago, USA, developed in the early part of the twentieth century (Gilgun, 1999, 2007). The ideas of conjectures, refutations, and reformulations that are part of DQA are based upon the work of Karl Popper (1969).

DQA and the Scientific Method

Deductive qualitative analysis follows the scientific method, which involves proposing a theory, testing it, and then revising it based on results of the test (Popper, 1969). Another way to think about the scientific method is the following. Science is based upon procedures of conjectures in the form of hypotheses, refutation through the process of testing hypotheses for their fit with phenomena, and reformulation when the hypotheses that are tested do not fit phenomena (Gilgun, 2005a; Popper, 1969).

In DQA as in the scientific method in general, researchers consider the initial theory to be preliminary. The purpose of DQA is to come up with a better theory than researchers had constructed at the outset (Gilgun, 2005c). Indeed, the production of new, more useful hypotheses is the goal of science.

The Terminology of DQA

The terminology of DQA can be confusing. Researchers refer to the initial theoretical framework in various ways, such as a preliminary theory, an analytic framework, a theoretical model, a preliminary model, and the initial or.7 preliminary hypothesis or hypotheses.

The final product of DQA also has more than one name, including tested and refined theory or model, the improved model, and the final model. Whatever terms researchers use, DQA is based on the idea that "final" theory is not final at all, but tentative and subject to revision when there is evidence to do so (Gilgun, 2005c).

The term *hypothesis* can also be a confusing term in DQA. In the present context, hypotheses are statements of relationships among concepts. Any hypothesis is composed of at least two concepts and a statement of the relationship between them, such as the hypothesis that Clever Foxes (a concept) know exactly what they are doing (a concept). Concepts in DQA serve sensitizing purposes, meaning they help researchers see aspects of phenomena that might not otherwise have noticed.

This is both their strength and weakness, strength precisely because they enlighten and thus serve as lenses with which to view the world. The sensitizing purposes of concepts also represent weakness because they may blind researchers to other significant aspects of phenomena (Blumer, 1954/1969). Thus researchers may only pay attention to data that support their assumptions and ignore other important data. It is easy enough to find material that upholds one's assumptions, but this is not science.

Negative Case Analysis

Researchers avoid finding what they intend to find through the conscious search for evidence that contradicts their emerging findings. This requires a form of sampling called negative case analysis, which involves the search for data that adds additional dimensions or even contradicts researchers' emerging understandings. Negative case analysis fits well with the ideas of conjectures, refutations, and reformulations (Gilgun, 2005c).

Another way to think of sampling in deductive qualitative analysis is the idea of maximum variability, where researchers attempt to sample a wide variety of cases in order to arrive at a comprehensive theory. The sampling is purposeful in that researchers intentionally select cases that represent a wide variety of types. The result is a set of exemplars that are representative of the many variations.

In the present study, I sought maximum variability in the selection of cases, and the sample thus achieved heterogeneity. However, given the likelihood of the protean nature of BS, it is likely that other variations not accounted for in the sample actually do exist. Thus, any theory based on DQA is flexible, intended to be modifiable if a new situation or case calls for flexibility. Such are the challenges and pleasures of scientific endeavors.

DQA AND ANALYTIC INDUCTION

Deductive qualitative analysis (DQA) is an updating of analytic induction (AI) which is a research method associated with the Chicago School of Sociology (Bulmer, 1984; Gilgun 2005c, 2007). Like DQA, AI starts with a preliminary theory, tests the theory on cases, selects samples based on negative case analysis, and continually revises the theory according to what researchers find through their analysis of cases.

Some researchers who used AI stated that their findings were universal, meaning that they fit every case they investigated, not that they fit every specific instance of an entire class of phenomena. Those who originated AI recognized that their "final" theories are in fact tentative, subject to revision when new evidence comes to light (Cressey, 1953).Analytic induction went through a long period of disrepute because some methodologists misunderstood its premises. For instance, these methodologists thought that by "universal" researchers using AI meant that their findings were general laws, applicable across time, place, and persons (Gilgun, 2005c). In fact, as stated, those who used AI saw findings as subject to revision.

The Ecological Fallacy

Methodologists also misunderstood how to use the findings of AI. They correctly noted that findings are not applicable to an entire population. Researchers who developed AI recognized this and instead expected findings to be tested for their fit with new situations. They knew that the next case could force modification of any theory they were in the process of testing and developing.

Any findings from research, including findings based on true random samples cannot be assumed to fit any one individual, even someone who was part of the sample on which the findings were developed. What is true for a group may not be true of individuals who compose that group. Assuming that group findings fit individual situations has a name: the ecological fallacy. Any finding, whether resulting from case studies, an experiment, or a survey, must be tested for fit in applied settings (Cronbach, 1975)

Analytic induction, like DQA, has as its purpose theory-building and cannot answer questions about distribution of qualities within a population, such as how many people will vote Democratic, Republican, Green, Independent, otherwise, or not at all.

Many of the ideas connected to AI are also part of DQA, but DQA elaborates upon many of these ideas and adds new ones. For instance, those who have created AI gave scant attention to the various types of initial hypotheses with which researchers begin their studies, nor do they define such terms as theory, model, and hypotheses. They provided little guidance as to how to incorporate previous research and theory into the development of the initial hypotheses and into emerging findings.

These researchers appear not to have considered ideas related to the sensitizing nature of concepts that is so important in testing and revising hypotheses. They did not connect negative case analysis with Popper's ideas of conjectures and refutations nor with ideas of maximum variability. These are some of the elaborations that the present author developed to create DQA and that are accounted for in the present investigation and in articles previously cited.

Deductive qualitative analysis (DQA) also states clearly how important it is for researchers to begin qualitative, case-based research with a preliminary theory that also serves as a conceptual framework. If they do not, they have little chance of having proposals funded by sponsoring agencies or accepted by dissertation committees.

Some researchers fear that they will find what they expect to find if they begin their research with hypotheses (Glaser, 1973; Glaser & Strauss, 1967; Strauss & Corbin, 1998). These fears are well founded. In response, DQA offers the principles of conjectures, refutations, and reformulations to counteract these tendencies and, furthermore, shows how negative case analysis represents a means of refuting previous conjectures.

Finally, analytic induction is not induction at all, but a combination of induction and deduction. For example, if a horse owner sees a gooey yellow substance in the corner of her horse's eye, she uses both induction and deduction to conclude that her horse has an eye infection. She has prior understanding of pus as an indicator of infection. Prior knowledge is a source of deductive reasoning. She sees the yellow substance in her horse's eye and concludes the horse has an eye infection based on prior knowledge (induction).

The horse owner did not have a prior framework in mind when she looked at the horse's eye, but when she saw the yellow substance, she immediately thought of eye infection. In this instance, she began with no prior framework but immediately called one up when she saw the substance in the corner of the eye.

Had someone told her that her horse appeared to have an eye infection, she would have looked at the eye with that hypothesis in mind. If she had seen the yellow, soft substance, she would have tentatively concluded that the hypothesis fit the situation. Whether she looked at the eye with a hypothesis in mind (deductive) or with no hypothesis (which would lead to inductive reasoning), she would have sought further confirmation of her hypothesis, no matter the starting point, by contacting a veterinarian and having the vet inspect the eye. If the hypothesis were to be confirmed, then action would follow.

The vet would sell the horse owner medication and the horse owner would apply it to the horse's eye as directed. If the vet were correct in her conclusion, and if she prescribed the correct medication, and if the owner applied the medication as directed and in the correct dose, then the horse's eye would clear up. Results would confirm or disconfirm the hypothesis.

Preliminary Theory as a Deductive Approach

Deductive qualitative analysis (DQA) begins with the construction of a preliminary theory that is tested and refined as a result of an analysis. The theory also serves a sensitizing function, as discussed. When researchers seek evidence to disconfirm or to discover new dimensions of their emerging hypotheses, they often take inductive approaches as described above.

This means they may set aside their prior theory as much as they can and attempt to be open to new aspects of phenomena under investigation. They do not know exactly what they are looking for other than they want to find something different from what they already think they know.

SUMMARY

Deductive qualitative analysis typically is used to test and refine hypotheses. Data are transcripts of interviews, fieldnotes from observations, and other texts, such as case records, photographs, and videos that others have constructed. The present investigation shows that a serious scientific endeavor can treat a difficult subject with humor and also can make scientific knowledge available to a wide audience and not simply to other academics. Finally, I spoofed social science research in my development and testing of a theory of BS. I did this out of affection for social scientists and their endeavors. May this book help us all to lighten up while at the same time stimulate researchers to undertake serious investigations of difficult topics.

REFERENCES

Blumer, Herbert. (1954/1969). What is wrong with social theory? In Herbert Blumer (1969/1986), *Symbolic interactionism.* (pp. 140-152) Berkeley: University of California Press. Originally published in Vol. XIX in *The American Sociological Review.*

Bulmer, Martin (1984). *The Chicago School of Sociology: Institutionalization, diversity, and the rise of sociological research*. Chicago: University of Chicago Press.

Cressey, Donald (1953). *Other people's money*. Belmont, CA: Wadsworth.

Cronbach, Lee J. (1975). Beyond the two disciplines of scientific psychology. *American Psychologist, 30,* 116-127.

Gilgun, Jane F. (1999).Methodological pluralism and qualitative family research. In Suzanne K. Steinmetz, Marvin B. Sussman, and Gary W. Peterson (Eds.), *Handbook of Marriage and the Family* (2nd ed.) (pp. 219-261). New York: Plenum.

Gilgun, Jane F. (2005a). "Grab" and good science: Writing up the results of qualitative research. *Qualitative Health Research*, 15(2), 256-262.

Gilgun, Jane F. (2005b). Lighten up! The citation dilemma in qualitative research. *Qualitative Health Research, 15(5) 721-725.*

Gilgun, Jane F. (2005c). Qualitative research and family psychology. *Journal of Family Psychology, 19(1),* 40-50.

Gilgun, Jane F. (2006). The four cornerstones of qualitative research. *Qualitative Health Research, 16(3),* 436-443.

Gilgun, Jane F. (2007, November). The legacy of the Chicago School of Sociology for Family Theory Building. Paper presented at the Pre-Conference Workshop on Theory Construction and Research Methodology, annual conference of the National Council on Family Relations, November 7.

Glaser, Barney. (1978). *Theoretical sensitivity.* Mill Valley, CA: Sociology Press.

Glaser, Barney & Anselm A. Strauss (1967). *The discovery of grounded theory.* Chicago: Aldine.

Popper, Karl (1969). *Conjectures and refutations: The growth of scientific knowledge.* London: Routledge and Kegan Paul.

Strauss, Anselm, & Juliet Corbin (1998). *Basics of qualitative research: Techniques and procedures for developing grounded theory* (2nd ed.). Thousand Oaks, CA: Sage.

ENDNOTES

Part One:

Developing a Theory of BS

Introduction

When someone dumps on us and then tries to cover up,
a typical response is "You shit!"

An example of unkind deeds and cover-ups (BS) in regard to criminal matters is a father who commits incest on his daughter. When the daughter tells her mother who in turn calls the police, the father covers up by saying that the mother refuses to have sex with him and the daughter made passes at him. He succeeds at BS when others believe him and blame the mother and daughter. In some cases, mothers and daughters accept the blame because they have internalized blame-the-victim beliefs. Blame-the-victim is a long-established cover-up.

The same scenario is at work for survivors of marital, date, and street rape. Women and men who survive intimate partner violence often are looked down upon as if there is something wrong with them for being beaten.

Blame the victim in sexual assault cases has a long history. See Karl Abraham, *The Experiencing of Sexual Trauma as a Form of Sexual Activity.* In Karl Abraham, *Selected Papers on Psycho-Analysis* (London: Hogarth, 1942) first published in 1907; see also, L. Bender and A. Blau, The reaction of children to sexual relations with adults. *American Journal of Orthopsychiatry,* vol. 11, pp. 730-743, 1941; I. Kaufman, A. L. Peck, & C. K. Tagiuri, the family constellation and overt incestuous relations between father and daughter, *American Journal of Orthopsychiatry*, 1954, vol. 24, pp. 266-277; F. Revitch & R. Weiss. The pedophiliac offender, *Diseases of the Nervous System*, vol. 23, pp. 73-78, 1962.

Victims of sexual abuse and rape are silent out of fear that they will be held responsible. They can suffer enormously and take years to recover from shock and shame. See Patricia Francisco, *Telling: A Memoir of Rape and Recovery* (New York: Harper Collins, 1999) and Surinder Jaswal. Child and Adolescent Sexual Abuse in Health Facilities, *Indian Journal of Social Work,* vol. 66 , no. 4, pp. 395-413, 2005.

Other sources of my understandings of what it means to be a shit come from my job as a social worker. I have had direct experience with many children who have experienced abuse and neglect and perpetrators have refused to take responsibility for their behaviors. They prefer to let the children think they did something wrong and they deserved or caused their own abuse and neglect.

My work with survivors of sexual and physical assault provides additional background to the present investigation. Society assigns blame to survivors for their own assaults. What did she do to provoke it? Why didn't she kick him out? Why didn't she just leave? These examples hardly do justice to victim-blaming statements that shift attention from those who truly are responsible. Such a diversion of attention lets perpetrators off the hook. Then they are free to abuse someone else, or to re- abuse victims who are now silenced.

I wrote *On Being a Shit* while writing *Child Sexual Abuse: From Harsh Realities to Hope* that go into detail about the meanings of interpersonal violence to perpetrators.

Harry Frankfurt, a retired Princeton University professor of philosophy, scored a hit when he re-published as a book an essay he had written years earlier. See Harry G. Frankfurt, *On Bullshit*. (Princeton, NJ: Princeton University Press, 2005). http://press.princeton.edu/titles/7929.html Retrieved March 3, 2008. The book sold more than four hundred thousand copies by October 2006 and had been translated into twenty-five languages, according to an interview in the *New York Times Magazine* published on Sunday, October 22, 2006.

The use of the vernacular in serious writing has a long history in the English language. For example, more than six hundred years ago, Geoffrey Chaucer used several such terms in *The Canterbury Tales*, to great humorous effect, although he did not use the term *shit* as I do in the present book. Maeve Binchy, a best-selling contemporary Irish novelist, followed in Chaucer's footsteps and also used vernacular at key points in her book *Quentins* (New York: Signet, 2003) Furthermore, she used the word *shit* as I do: to designate a person (Don) who had committed unkind deeds and then successfully covered them up, at least for a time. She also used the word *bastard* to designate Don when he failed at being a shit. *Quentins* is available at http://www.amazon.com/Quentins-Maeve-Binchy/dp/0451209907 Retrieved March 3, 2008.

Besides using the vernacular to describe everyday behaviors, *On Being a Shit* is part of another trend. University professors in increasing numbers are writing books for the general public instead of writing to other researchers. An example is *The Sociopath Next Door*, a best-seller written by Harvard psychologist Martha Stout, who shows how sociopaths come across in everyday life so that readers can recognize them. Stout's book *The Sociopath Next Door* is available at http://www.randomhouse.com/broadway/catalog/display.pperl?isbn=9780767915823. Retrieved March 3, 2008. *On Being a Shit* uses the everyday word *shit* to describe persons who perform unkind deeds and cover-ups. Being a shit fits many different personality disorders, such as narcissistic, antisocial, and borderline, but fits people without such disorders, too, being an equal opportunity set of behaviors. The meanings of these words are mysterious, but everyone knows what being a shit means.

Good sources of information about cognitive neuroscience include Michael S. Gazzaniga, Richard B. Ivry, and George R. Mangun, *Cognitive Neuroscience: The Biology of the Mind* (New York: Norton, 2002); Joseph LeDoux, *The Synaptic Self: How Our Brains Become Who We Are.* (New York: Penguin, 2002); and Joseph LeDoux, *The Emotional Brain.* (New York: Simon & Schuster, 1996)

For further information on Popper, see Karl Popper, *Conjectures and Refutations: The Growth of Scientific Knowledge* (London: Routledge and Kegan Paul, 1969).

For details on deductive qualitative analysis (DQA), which is the name of the kind of theory-testing that I did, see Jane F. Gilgun, Qualitative Research and Family Psychology, *Journal of Family Psychology*, vol. 19, no. 1, pp4 0-50, 2005 and Jane F. Gilgun, Deductive Qualitative Analysis and Family Theory-Building. In Vern Bengston, Peggye Dillworth Anderson, Katherine Allen, Alan Acock, & David Klein (Eds.). *Sourcebook of Family Theory and Methods,* pp. 83-84. (Thousand Oaks, CA: Sage, 2004). Available at http://www.sagepub.com/refbooksProdDesc.nav?prodId=Book226285 Retrieved March 3, 2008.

Chapter Two

Shedding Light in Dark Places

Getting others to believe it is their fault
is the crowning achievement of being a shit

Chapters one and two of this book are based upon my professional experience, personal observations, and general knowledge of related research and theory. In addition, my personal and professional values of fair play are infused through this book. Building theory that has such a foundation is equivalent to two of the four cornerstones of evidence-based practice. It is important to build researchers' knowledge into their work.

In conducting research, whether theory-testing or not, it is important for researchers to have an understanding of how their personal and professional perspectives influence their findings. See Jane F. Gilgun, The four cornerstones of evidence-based practice in social work. *Research on Social Work Practice,* vol. 15, no. 1, pp. 52-61, 2005 and Jane F. Gilgun, Lived Experience, Reflexivity, and Research on Perpetrators of Interpersonal violence. *Qualitative Social Work*, vol. 7. no. 2 to be published June 2008.

In the story of the mastodon hunting party, readers may recognize the allusion to Dick Cheney's shooting of Harry Whittington on quail hunt at a Texas ranch in February 2006. I tell this story in more detail in chapter fourteen.

Chapter Three

Scholarly Inquiry into Origins
and Meanings of Being a Shit

BS differs
from related human conditions

This information on word origins and meanings of *shit* comes from many sources. See The *American Heritage Dictionary of the English Language.* (Boston: Houghton Mifflin, op. cit.; *Online Etymological Dictionary*, http://www.etymonline.com. Retrieved February 8, 2006; *The Shorter Oxford English Dictionary Based on Historical Principles* (3rd ed.). (Oxford, UK: Clarendon Press, 1966); *Wikipedia*, the free encyclopedia, http://en.wikipedia.org/wiki/Shit. Retrieved February 8, 2006; *Wiktionary*, a wiki-based open content dictionary, http://en.wiktionary.org wiki/shit. Retrieved February 8, 2006.

Scat, which means animal droppings, especially those of wild animals, is likely a cognate as well. The origins of *scat* are unclear, but a related word, *scatology,* which is the scientific study of excrement, is linked to the Greek *skat-* . Another meaning of scatology is interest in obscene material. Information on the origins of *scat* is from the *Mirriam-Webster On-Line Dictionary* at http://www.m-w.com/dictionary/scatology

The article on Pádraig Clancy is by Dermot Crowe, Tower of Strength, *Sunday Irish Independent*, July 15, 2007, p. 5.

Bush's use of the word *shit* was reported nationally and internationally. A good source is Jim Rutenberg. Bush's Policy Chit-Chat: Undiplomatic Prose. *New York Times* Tuesday, July 18, 2006. p. A6.

The *New York Times* columnist referred to in the text is Thomas L. Friedman, Order vs. Disorder, *New York Times*, July 19, 2006, p. A23. The Newsday cartoon was reprinted in the *Minneapolis Star Tribune* on July 23, 2006, on page AA5.

For more detail on the responses to Harry Frankfurt's use of the term *bullshit*, see Kenneth Baker, That's a Ton of Bull -- and That's No Lie. *San Francisco Chronicle*, April 17, 2005. http://www.sfgate.com/cgi-bin/article.cgi?file=/chronicle/archive/2005/04/17/RVGBTC5FK31. DTL. August 9, Retrieved August 9 2006; Fritz Lanham, On BS by Harry G. Frankfurt. *Houston Chronicle*, February 6, 2005. http://www.chron.com/disp/story.mpl/ae/books/reviews/3023401.html.Retrieved August 9, 2006; Peter Edin, Between Truth and Lies: An Unprintable Ubiquity, *New York Times*, February 14, 2005. http://select.nytimes.com/search/restricted/article?res=F20717F83 E5E0C778DDDAB0894DD404482 Retrieved August 9, 2006; Dwight Garner, Inside the List. *New York Times*, March 12, 2006. http://www. nytimes.com/2006/03/12/books/review/12tbr.html?ex=11552688 00 &en=91015d514401fd97&ei=5070. Retrieved August 9, 2006.

For an interview with Harry Frankfurt on his sequel to *On Bullshit*, see Deborah Solomon, Fighting Bull: The Princeton Philosopher Talks About his Latest Book, which Ivy League School is the World Capital of Bull— and Why Short Books are Better Than Long Ones. *New York Times Magazine*, October 21, 2006, p. 29.

See Eric Partridge for the notation that shit at one time was part of standard English. Eric Partridge, *A Dictionary of Slang and Unconventional English: Slang—Including the Language of the Underworld, Colloquialisms and Catch-Phrases, Solecisms and Catahreses, Nicknames, Vulgarisms and Such Americanisms as Have Been Naturalized* (New York: Macmillan, 1970).

For definitions of putz and schmuck see
http://www.thefreedictionary.com and
http://www.schmucku.com/definitition.html, both retrieved
December 12, 2007.

Sources for the discussion of the word *prick* include the on-
line *Etymological Dictionary*,
http://www.etymonline.com/index.php?
search=prick&searchmode=none. Retrieved May 20, 2006, and the
Sex Lexis, http://www.sex-lexis.com/Sex-Dictionary/pricksmith.
Retrieved May 20, 2006.

Chapter Four

Humbug, Bullshit, Lying, and Truthiness:
Conditions Related to BS

BS Differs From Related Human Conditions

Note that Frankfurt also discussed hot air, fakery, and
bluffing, which are beyond the scope of the present investigation but
could be of interest to scholars who wish to investigate other possible
variations of how human beings deceive themselves and others. One
could say that sociopaths are an extreme form of BS. The direct
quotes are from Frankfurt, op. cit., p. 16, p. 34, and p. 23, respectively.

Paul Ekman, Telling *Lies: Clues to Deceit in the Marketplace,
Politics, and Marriage* (New York: Norton, 2001).

Eliot Spitzer, who resigned as governor of New York in March
2008 after a scandal involving a female escort, prevaricated to his
wife and the U.S. Congress. According to *New York Times* columnist
Gail Collins, Spitzer bullied Congress into allowing him to testify
about bond insurance before the House financial services
subcommittee. Collins said Spitzer used his subcommittee testimony
as a "beard" to cover up his real purpose for being in Washington,
D.C., which was to have sex with a prostitute. See Gail Collins,
Unwelomce Surprises, *New York Times*, March 13, 2008, p. A23.

For further detail on the work of DePaulo see Bella M.
DePaulo and Deborah A. Kashy, Everyday Lies in Close and Casual
Relationships, *Journal of Personality and Social Psychology*, vol. 74, No.
1, 1998, pp. 63-79; Bella M. DePaulo, Chris Wetzel, R. Weylin
Sternglantz, and Molly J. Walker Wilson, Verbal and NonVerbal
Dynamics of Privacy, Secrecy and Deceit, *Journal of Social Issues*, vol.

59,No. 2, 2003, pp. 391-410; Bella M. DePaulo, Matthew E. Ansfield, Susan E. Kirkendol, and Joseph M. Boden, Serious Lies, *Basic and Applied Social Psychology*, Vol. 26, Nos. 2 & 3, pp. 147-167; Robin Marantz Henig, Lying, *New York Times* Magazine, Sunday, February 5, 2006, pp. 47-53, 76, 80, 83. The direct quotes are from DePaulo et al, op. cit., p. 159 and Henig, op. cit., p.83.

A good review of executive function is in Peter Anderson. Assessment and Development of Executive Function (EF) During Childhood. *Child Neuropsychology*, vol. 8, no. 2, pp. 71-82, 2002.

For information about the role of the cingulate gyrus in empathy see T. F. Farrow, Y. Zheng, I.D. Wilkinson, S.A. Spence, J.F. Deakin, N. Tarrier, P.D. Griffiths, & P.W. Woodruff. Investigating the Functional Anatomy of Empathy and Forgiveness. *Neuroreport*, vol. 12, no. 11, pp. 2433-2438, 2001.

For information on self-regulation, see Elizabeth LeCuyer & Gail M. Houck, Maternal Limit-Setting in Toddlerhood: Socialization Strategies for the Development of Self-Regulation, *Infant Mental Health Journal*, vol. 27, no. 4, pp. 344-370, 2006.

An extended discussion of the automatic activation of schemas is in John A. Bargh and Tanya L. Chartrand, The Unbearable Automaticity of Being. *American Psychologist*, . 54 no. 7, 1999, pp. 462-479. For more about schemas, see Timothy D. Wilson, *Strangers to Ourselves: Discovering The Adaptive Unconscious* (Cambridge, MA: Harvard University Press, 2002).

Malcolm Gladwell in *Blink*, (New York: Little Brown and Company, 2005) gives examples of how our expectations and predispositions can blind us even in the face of clear evidence that contradicts our views.

Chapter Five

A Preliminary Theory of BS

BS is impossible
without the consent of recipients

Erving Goffman coined the term *impression management* in his book *The Presentation of Self in Everyday Life* (Doubleday, 1959).

See Niccolo Machiavelli, *The Prince* (Robert M. Adams, trans. and ed.) (New York, Norton, 1977, first published 1513).

For the story on John Prin's views on what's at stake for Floyd Landis, see Gail Rosenblum, *Relationships: To Tell the Truth or Not? Minneapolis Star Tribune,* June 2, 2007. http://www.startribune. com/relationships/story/1219737-p2.html Retrieved June 2, 2007.

For more on the moral imagination, see Alexander McCall Smith *The Sunday Philosophy Club* (New York: Pantheon, 2004), p. 110.

In many ways, we human beings are strangers to ourselves. Much of what motivates us and gets us through the day happens automatically and outside of our awareness. This is fortunate. If we had to think about the wisdom of getting out of the way of a speeding car, we would lose valuable time and be hurt or killed. If we had to think about every step involved in waking up, getting out of bed, and brushing our teeth, we would be stuck in slow motion. Therefore, many of the automatically activated mental maps or schemas that are encoded in brain circuits are essential. See Bargh and Chartrand, cited earlier, and Wilson, cited earlier.

For information about truthiness, see the website of the American Dialect Society at http://www.americandialect.org/ Words_of_the_Year_2005.pdf. Retrieved November 21, 2007. An informative article is Colbert Fights for Truthiness, *Language Log*, January 10, 2006. http://www.itre.cis.upenn.edu/~my/1anguagelog/archives/02752.h tml. Retrieved November 21, 2007.

Part Two:
Testing a Theory of BS on Stories
from Everyday Life

Will the theory hold?

The story about the son and his father's car was broadcast on Car Talk, National Public Radio, broadcast on July 21, 2006 on Minnesota Public Radio.

Anthony's story is from Lynn Johnston, For Better or for Worse, *Minneapolis Star Tribune*, Tuesday, April 25, 2006, p. E4 and April 26, 2006, p. E6.

The citation for the book on coal mine cover-ups is Erik Reece, *Lost Mountain* (New York: Penguin, 2006).

It is possible that some behaviors are so callous that enactors have earned the status of shit of the bastard variety, meaning their cover-ups work, but their behaviors are so terrible that no way can the word *shit* fit. The term *shit* of the bastard variety may well fit the behaviors of perpetrators of child sexual abuse and other kinds of felony-level violence, including white collar crime. Definitions are important in social science. As is true in social science in general, I am sharing my definitions of terms so that readers know what I mean by them. Readers may have their own definitions, but it is important to know how I am using these terms in developing a theory of BS so that readers can follow the logic of my thought.

For the story of Laura and Sabrina, see Richard Zitrin and Carol M. Langford, *The Moral Compass of the American Lawyer* (New York, Ballantine, 1999).

For the story and Jamie and Hamish, see M.C. Beaton, *Death of a Scriptwriter* (New York: Mysterious, 1998).

For the story of Heather and her boyfriend, See Heather Fenby, Mélange á Trois: Me, Him…and the Stuff. The *New York Times*, February 5, 2006.

For responses to Heather's story, see V.K. Moss, Send Him to a Mountain, *New York Times*, February12, 2006. and Jennifer V. Hughes, She Thinks She's Abusive? *New York Times*, February 12, 2006.

The story of Ella and Don is in Maeve Binchy's novel *Quentins* (New York: Signet, 2003)

Another instance of a man who wanted two women is in Grace Glueck's review of Michael Winter's biography of Rockwell Kent, an artist. Grace Glueck, Books of The Times: The Great Why, Calamitous Year in the Life of a Philandering Artist, *New York Times* Book Review, February 8, 2006. Retrieved September 17, 2006. http://www.nytimes.com/2006/02/08/books/08glue.html?ex=1158 638400&en=4944dc3e2bcc510d &ei=5070

The quotes from Binchy, cited earlier, are on pages 87, 88, and 418.

I used many sources for the scenario of the Dick Cheney shooting of Harry Whittington. See Anne E. Kornblut, Cheney Shoots Fellow Hunter in Mishap on a Texas Ranch. *New York Times*, February 13, 2006. The article was written on Sunday, February 12, the day after Dick shot Harry and published the following day, on Monday, February 13. http://www.nytimes.com/2006/02/13/politics/13cheney.html? r=1 &sq=Dick%20Shoots%20Fellow%20Hunter&st=nyt&adxnnl=1&oref =slogin&scp=1&adxnnlx=1203272077-0vOevwisAvglJDZIUVFe/Q. Retrieved February 17, 2008.

To read an interview the vice president gave to Brit Hume of Fox News about his role in the shooting and the aftermath, see http://www.whitehouse.gov/news/releases/2006/ 02/20060215-3.html

For reports on the hunting accident, see Ralph Blumenthal. Timeline of Dick's Mishap, *International Herald Tribune Americas*, February 16, 2006. http://www.iht.com/articles/2006/02/16/ america/web.0216timeline.php. Retrieved May 25, 2006; Robert Paul Reyes, Harry Whittington Apologizes To Vice President Dick Cheney. American Chronicle. February 19, 2006 http://americanchronicle.com. Retrieved March 31, 2006.; David Usborne. Man Shot by Cheney Says "Accidents Will Happen." *Independent Online*, February 18, 2006. http://news.independent.co.uk/world/americas/article346138.ece Retrieved April 15, 2006. See also, Robert Paul Reyes, Harry Whittington Apologizes to Vice President Dick Cheney. *American Chronicle.* http://www.americanchronicle.com/articles/viewArticle.asp?articleI D=6047. Retrieved March 31, 2006.

For discussions of the rules of hunting, see Timothy J. Burger, How Did Dick Cheney Break the No. 1 Rule of Hunting? For Veteran Sportsmen Like the Vice President, Safety is a Core Value. *Time Magazine Online*, April 17, 2006. http://www.time.com/time/nation/article/0,8599,1159061,00.html. Retrieved April 17, 2006; Texas Park and Wildlife Department, Shooting Safety Rules: Rules Hunters Can Live By...Ten Commandments of Shooting Safety http://www.tpwd.state.tx.us/ learning/ huntereducation/ hotsafe.html; American Gun Safety Foundation, Gun Safety Program. http://www.agsfoundation.com/ safety/ hunting.html#identify. Retrieved April 17, 2006. For a joke months later, See Maureen Dowd, Fetch, Heel, Stall, *New York Times*, Sunday, July 30, 2006. http://select.nytimes.com/2006/07/29/opinion/29dowd.html? r=1 &oref=login. Retrieved July 31, 2006.

For the September 2007 interview of Clarence Thomas with Steve Kroft on 60 Minutes, see Clarence Thomas: The Justice Nobody Knows. http://www.cbsnews.com/stories/2007/09/27/60minutes/main33 05443.shtml. Retrieved December 5, 2007. For the 1991 Hill-Thomas controversy, see Anita Hill-Clarence Thomas Hearings. The Museum of Broadcast Communications.

http://www.museum.tv/archives/etv/H/htmlH/hill-thomas/hill-thomas.htm and An Outline of the Anita Hill and Clarence Thomas Controversy. http://chnm.gmu.edu/courses/122/hill/hilloutline2.htm. Retrieved December 5, 2007. Thomas's book is *My Grandfather's Son*, published by Harper in 2007.

For a story on Alberto Gonzales, see "Nothing to Hide," Gonzales Insists Before Hearing, *New York Times*, April 16, 2007. http://www.nytimes.com/2007/04/16/Washington/16attorneys.html?pagewanted=2&r=1. Retrieved December 27, 2007.

For a report on Karl Rove's TV appearance after the announcement of his resignation see Alessandra Stanley, THE TV WATCH; Rove Talks: If Mistakes Were Made, They Weren't His. *New York Times*, August 20, 2007. http://select.nytimes.com/search/restricted/article?res=FB0E16FE3. Retrieved August 28, 2007.

Valerie Plame Wilson wrote a book called Fair *Game, My Life as a Spy, my Betrayal by the White House*. New York: Simon & Schuster, 2007. Available at http://www.simonsays.com/content/book.cfm?tab=1&pid=591369. Retrieved March 3, 2008.

Part Three

Applications of the Theory to Stories
of Coming Clean

For the story of the two sisters and the painting, see Frank Gannon. The Funny Pages: A Family Heirloom. *New York Times Magazine.* March 26, 2006, p. 28.

For the story of Billy Pittman, see Joseph Duarte, Texas Suspends Receiver Pittman for Three Games, *The Houston Chronicle*, September 1, 2007. http://www.chron.com/CDA/archives/archive.mpl?id=2007_441. Retrieved January 4, 2008.

For a story about Harry Dent, see David Stout, Harry Dent, an Architect of Nixon 'Southern Strategy', Dies at 77, *New York Times*, October 2, 2007, p. C13. http://www.nytimes.com/2007/10/02/us/02dent.html?scp=2&sq=Harry+Dent&st=nyt. Retrieved December 27, 2007.

For the story of the drug company, see OxyContin Maker and Executives Plead Guilty to Misleading Public, *Boston Herald,* May 11, 2007, by the Associated Press. http://business.bostonherald.com/businessNews/view.bg?articleid=1000697&format=&page=2. Retrieved May 13, 2007. See also, Barry Meier. Narcotic Maker Guilty of Deceit Over Marketing *New York Times*, May 11, 2007. http://www.nytimes.com/2007/05/11/business/11drug.html?pagewanted=2&_r=1. Retrieved May 13, 2007.

For an account of Paul Wolfowitz's resignation see Statements of Executive Directors and President Wolfowitz, May 17, 2007 http://web.worldbank.org/WBSITE/EXTERNAL/NEWS/0.cotentMDK:21339650~menuPK:34463~pagePK:34370~piPK:34424~theSitePK:4607,00.html . Retrieved June 3, 2007.

For an article that shows how often politicians use the phrase "mistakes were made," see John M. Broder. Familiar Fallback for Officials:" Mistakes Were Made," *New York Times*, http://www.nytimes.com/2007/03/14/washington/14mistakes.html?_r=1&oref=slogin.

For stories about Oprah Winfrey and James Frey see, The Man Who Conned Oprah, The Smoking Gun, http://www.thesmokinggun.com/archive/0104061jamesfrey1.html. Retrieved May 15, 2007. Also, Editorial: On Oprah's Couch, *New York Times*, January 27, 2006. http://select.nytimes.com/search/restricted/article?res=F30F11FC3A5B0C748EDDA80894DE404482. Retrieved June 2, 2007 Other stories are by Michael Conlon. Author Frey Admits Fiction, Oprah Apologizes. by Reuters. January 26, 2007. Retrieved May 15, 2007. http://www.redorbit.com/news/entertainment/371034/author_frey_admits_fictions_oprah_apologizes/index.html#. Oprah Interviews Author Frey. Oprah Winfrey Show. Air Date: January 26, 2006 http://www2.oprah.com/tows/slide/200601/20060126/slide_20060126_350_204.html. Retrieved May 13, 2007.

For stories about Jimmy Carter's criticism of the George W. Bush administration, see Steve Holland, Bush Plays Down Jimmy Carter Criticism. http://www.washingtonpost.com/wp-dyn/content/article/2007/05/21/AR2007052100767.html. Retrieved May 28, 2007; John Nichols, Who's Afraid of Jimmy Carter?

George Bush. *The Nation.*
http://thenation.com/blogs/thebeat?pid=197253. Retrieved
November 11, 2007; Jimmy Carter Backtracks on Calling Bush
Administration Worst in U.S. History.
http://www.foxnews.com/printer_printer_friendly_story/0,3566,274
1,00.html. Retrieved November 11, 2007.

Part Four

Discussion and Conclusions,
or Where Do We Go From Here?

For stories on Allen Raymond, see Adam Cohen, A Tale of
Political Dirty Tricks Makes the Case for Election Reform, *New York
Times*, January 1, 2008.
http://www.nytimes.com/2008/01/01/opinion/01tue3.html?em&ex
=1100336400&en=d72c4, Retrieved January 2, 2008; Jonathan Finer,
Former GOP Consultant Sentenced to Prison. Washingtonpost.com.
February 9, 2005. www.washingtonpost.com/wp-
dyn/articles/A9149-2005Feb8.html. Retrieved January 2, 2008;
Michael Kranish, Fallen star blames self, GOP. *The Boston Globe,*
http://www.boston.com/news/nation/Washington/articles/2006/0
6/10/fallen_star_blames_self.... Retrieved January 2, 2008.

Raymond Allen's book, written with Ian Spiegelman, *How to
Rig an Election: Confessions of a Republican Operative* was published
in January 2008 by Simon and Schuster and available at
http://www.simonsays.com/content/book.cfm?tab=1&pid=592156&
er=9781416552222. Retrieved March 3, 2008.

Perpetrators of child sexual abuse often express relief when
their abuse comes to light. George (not his real name) said about
turning himself in to the police, "It was a relief. Even as crappy as it
was and as much as it hurt and it's scary and painful and everything,
to finally have that weight lifted off of my shoulders, to let go of that
horrible secret, was incredible."

For those who are afraid to entertain the notion that they
could do something wrong and even harmful, remember the Hmong
saying, "The spirit will catch you if you fall"

Readers familiar with Twelve Step programs may recognize
the phrase "Wisdom is knowing what to overlook."

About the Author

Jane F. Gilgun, Ph.D., LICSW, is professor, School of Social Work, University of Minnesota, Twin Cities, USA. She is the author of a related book called *Child Sexual Abuse: From Harsh Realities to Hope* available at Google Books, iBooks, Kindle, and other internet booksellers.

Professor Gilgun does research on the meanings of violence to perpetrators, the development of violent behaviors, and how persons overcome adversities. She got the idea for *On Being a Shit* from this research. After years of interviewing people who had committed seriously harmful crimes and then tried to cover them up, she began to see that many other people committed comparatively mild versions of unkind deeds and cover-ups.

She has published many scholarly articles and now also writes books, articles, and blogs for the general public.

Professor Gilgun has a Ph.D. in child and family studies from Syracuse University, a master's in social work from the University of Chicago, and a licentiate in family studies and sexuality from the Catholic University of Louvain, Belgium. In addition, she has a bachelor's and master's degree in English literature with a concentration in poetry for both degrees. She is a licensed independent clinical social worker.

Her interests include her horses, Padron's Elegante and Finn MacCool, who are mother and son, her dog Jazz, gardening, photography, cooking, the arts, and spending time County Leitrim and other border counties of the Republic of Ireland.